WITHDRAWN

Advance Praise for *Old Age in the New Age. . .*

"*Old Age in the New Age* is an eclectic romp through the New Age 'mind fields.' Here Stone is as comfortable discussing ketones as she is *cveching* about how some people spend their lives. She shows us the folly of those who continue to devour emotional placebos only to return to square one after all the hype, the sessions, and the fasting, to say, 'Now what?'"

—Bruno Respigna
The Albuquerque Journal

"Here is a marvelous antidote for the pernicious virus of self-importance that often afflicts New Agers and their fellow travelers in the holistic health, utopian, and millennial movements. Arlene Stone's wit is sharp yet affectionate, and she really knows her stuff. Indeed, if the new paradigm is to survive, it must embrace the balanced clear-headedness and down-to-earth levity of *Old Age in the New Age*."

—Richard Polese
Co-compiler, *Peace Pilgrim*
President, New Mexico Book Association
Author of *Discovering Dixie*

"Stone, an irreverent, irresistibly comic crone, is to be commended for her originality with the scope and complexity of her subjects. The glossary alone is worth the price, current and comprehensive. The apparent ease and freshness of her writing will surely delight the reader. I heartily recommend *Old Age in the New Age*."

—Dorothy Perron, PhD
Gerontologist
Director, Seniors Reaching Out

WITHDRAWN

Old Age
IN THE
New Age

Old Age
IN THE
New Age

IRREVERENT REFLECTIONS ON MILLENNIAL MADNESS

Arlene Stone

Optimist
Press
Santa Fe, New Mexico

Published by: **Optimist Press**
PO Box 2880
Santa Fe, NM 87504-2880

Editor: Ellen Kleiner
Book design and typography: Richard Harris
Cover design: Tracey Gallegos, Alphagraphics

A Blessingway book

Copyright © 1999 by Arlene Stone

All rights reserved. No part of this publication may be reproduced in any form whatsoever without written permission from the publisher, except for brief quotations embodied in literary articles or reviews.

Printed in the United States of America on acid-free recycled paper

Publisher's Cataloging-in-Publication Data

Stone, Arlene.
    Old age in the New Age ; irreverent reflections on
    millennial madness / Arlene Stone. — 1st ed.
    p. cm.
    Includes bibliographical references.
    LCCN: 98-93553
    ISBN: 09640771-1-6

    1. New Age movement. 2. New Age persons. 3. Aged.
    I. Title.

BP605.N48S76 1999   299.93
                                       QB198-1528

10 9 8 7 6 5 4 3 2 1

Contents

Introduction

On the eve of the next thousand-year cycle, there is a spirited frenzy in the air. Call it millennial madness. New Agers count down the months to minutes while I'm trying to deal with the incursions and intrusions of Old Age, a young head on an aging body. My feet are stuck in concrete while others Sufi dance through the lotus. I watch the New Agers jogging, running, even hobbling despite their varicose veins, bypasses, heart transplants, and prostheses. At times I don't feel ready for the human potential movement, the unconditional *love of the universal*. When I feel fragmented, I resist like a Greek fury the mere suggestion of harmonic convergence. Nor can I deal, when I've glued my pieces back together, with the idea that the holy Bible is an extraterrestrial transmission.

Admittedly, I'm irreverent. I may also be as unconvertible as any Jew who yearns for rose gardens in Mecca or Medina while settling for stagnant ponds in the New Jerusalem. I come from a long string of peddlers, from Sarai of the so-called second gender, who took more than nine decades to reproduce.

New Age is a hungry canine catching up with me, a hound of heaven or hell, while Old Age beckons from an alley like a dirty old man. If death is the adventure New Agers proclaim it is, the light should be radiant at the end of the dark tunnel. Yet, here I am standing on the sidelines, a wallflower of the nineties, while the parade of the joyous passes: gurus with their publishers and followers, tanning and anti-tanning salonists, drill-less dentists and knifeless plastic surgeons, nutrition faddists, body-workers, TV swamis, educators, scientists, politicians.

We can't run from Old Age . . . or New Age either, which began on the radical fringe and has been creeping toward the center, a national fad as Solomonic as the new physics, its parts as antiquated as the bearded seer. So I am led to examine what some revere as the unexaminable.

The twin goals of this book are to inform and to entertain. To assist in informing, there is a glossary at the back, along with a recommended reading list. Consequently, this book is for both the uninitiated and the converted, for seniors as well as baby boomers and even youths daring enough to approach the precipice of old age and glimpse into an abyss that can be as fertile as a green valley. Youth, after all, has been in the forefront of New Age, digging up old seeds from the Medes to grow new mung beans in Nebraska.

The book's tone is alternately serious and satirical. It aims at a quick overview of New Age that will raise as many questions as are bearable, while urging you to select what is usable and dispose of anything unworthy of recycling. It offers a short sprint across a toe-stubbing beach pricked with flotsam and jetsam.

Warning: This is not a how-to book. A plethora of practical instruction manuals currently in the public arena guide their readers toward Nirvana with tips on diet, exercise, ritual, and sex. This book is, instead, a protest against the New-Age-will-save-you seers, an attempt to prod you to reexamine their exhortations about perfection with a more commonsense personal agenda. The chapters address various contemporary issues through a writing technique that interweaves narrative and first-person accounts with more linear analyses of such topics as the history of healing and virtual reality, mixed with humorous interludes to give your mind and conscience a rest. These twists and turnings mirror an inherent cry against the tunnel thinking and linear "solutions" aimed at aging.

Writing from a female point of view, as that is what I know best, I leave it to men writers to have their own say on such aging issues as male weight gain and loss of hair, sexual potency, and credibility. For now, I trust there are men curious to read about what women are experiencing.

Having been raised in the suburbs of a Talmudic tradition that enjoys, as Buddhists do, verbal argument, I have tried throughout to resist a wise-aleck stance. In the face of millennial angst, it may not seem appropriate to prick the hot air balloons designed to rejoin members of our species with humanoids far out beyond Mars. I say rejoin to acknowledge the belief of some that humans bred with high fliers from outer space back in the days of the Sumerian king Ashurbanipal.

As poet Alan Dugan wrote, "frivolity is the mask of despair." Yet who can despair amid Deepak Chopra's New Age meadows "splashed with daisies"?

Part One

Geeks and Gurus

Chapter One

An Aquarian Millenarian

What Is Aquarian Consciousness?

All I know is, I haven't got it. When I find it, I'll be a millenarian. I'm giving up Powerball as an opiate of the masses. I won't sneak into the Indian casino at Pojoaque anymore on a Sunday morning instead of going to church. True, I'll miss the secondhand smoke, but why gamble away my stake in the hereafter? Forget being a millionaire; I've got to start collecting Aquarian chips. The nuclear age has had it. The Beach Boys announced this, but I wasn't listening. I was too high on liberation, shaking my rear end in all-night discos while gray hairs were creeping onto my New Age scalp.

Now the 1990s have caught me dozing. How can I sleep while Rome burns? I can still hear the tune, although most of the words escape me: "The Age of Aquarius, the Age of Aquarius . . ." What did I think we were singing about? I was too high on vodka tonics to find out. But God bless the 1960s, here is the age I was waiting for and I, who thought myself with it, am locked out.

Is Aquarian utopian? It's certainly mystical, like the Hebrew Eremites.

But that was Masada, where they threw themselves off a cliff to escape the Romans marching up a ramp from the Dead Sea. Is Aquarius an escape valve for martyrs? There must be more to it than that.

Conspiracy Theory

Marilyn Ferguson's *The Aquarian Conspiracy: Personal and Social Transformation in the 1980s* was a frontier-crashing book in its time. It seems unfair to look for holes in a sieve nearly two decades old, like skipping ahead to the end of a mystery novel to find out who done it. But that's the fate of the written word.

What does Aquarius signify? The water bearer in the ancient zodiac, symbolizing flow and the quenching of thirst, and apparently spurring on a great conspiracy. Frankly, I can see him in the night sky only as a blur. My long-distance vision is going, going, gone. So what if it's the eleventh sign of the zodiac? What's that got to do with me? I'm a Taurean, bull-headed. I'd cut off my nose to spite my face. Though I'm hardly horny anymore, I can't go back and change when I was born. Nor can I blame my parents and be New Age.

The Truth According to Ferguson

Ferguson's Aquarius heralds the replacing of our dark and violent Piscean millennium with a new age of love and light, the mind's true liberation, social and personal transformation, individual life as revolution, the unleashing of creativity and initiative. This energy fans out for conservation, against the exploitation of natural resources and humans. Such awakenings are attributed to the widening gulf between culture and belief.

According to Ferguson, Aquarius represents a paradigm shift, a new way of thinking about old problems. "By its larger perspective," she tells us, "it transforms traditional knowledge and the stubborn new observations, reconciling their apparent contradictions."[1] Aquarius is the melting swan of Lohengrin, mind's latest table decoration.

Aquarians, descendants of transcendentalists who searched for inner freedom, have founded human potential centers, including one at Esalen, in California's Big Sur area. Here, probing intellects have met for over thirty years to massage Oriental and Occidental values, visions, and consciousness.

In the Aquarian Age we move through stress to transformation.

Am I Ready to Give up Stress?

Am I ready to toss away a teething ring with proven materiality in order to rub my gums on clouds of insubstantiality? Am I ready to change my changing? Isn't it enough that since menopause I can't sleep, let alone dream? Forget the night sweats, the tightness, the painful internals.

Aquarians by birth are now welcoming Aquarians by adoption: a one-time offer. In an age of "the change of change," am I to remain a spiritual orphan? Better get in before they close the pearly gates. I visualize a waiting tram with pastel lighting, blue and pink, with Albert what's-his-name and Meryl Streep.

What am I getting into? I hope it's not a spaceship with Roswell aliens looking to get even, outsiders ulcer prone like me, and disagreeable. That can't be it. New Age is a rainbow. I've seen it on greeting cards and billboards.

What does the Age of Aquarius really mean?

And What *Is* the Aquarian Conspiracy?

Marilyn Ferguson uses the term to refer to a conscious attempt to reform Western culture. Can I aspire to the Golden Age without reading Aquarian novels or joining a nativistic health cult? By Golden Age I don't mean Old Age. We're talking here of dawn, not the twilight of the gods.

We're talking of the truth of being, as the guru Ram Dass would say. We're talking of nothing less than my *dharma*. Or as René Daumal writes, "One climbs, one sees, one descends; one sees no longer but one has seen. . . . When one can no longer see, one can at least still know."[2] Does this refer to the shamanic journey to the summit or to incipient cataracts? If the latter, are the cataracts my spirit guides?

Other Guides

The New Age landscape vibrates with guides. In *Santa Fe Sun*, a New Mexico periodical, a group of local women call themselves "The Path of

Light." A "psychic & spirit guide" offers channeled readings. A "psychic intuitive" refers to herself as an "animal communicator." My favorite guide is the "Angelic Communicator Automatic."

I confess that I'm having too much trouble with humans to make angels or animals top priority. I do wish to communicate better with dogs so that I don't turn to Jell-O when my parking car is surrounded by a barking German shepherd and two territorial Dobermans.

Actually, the only animal communication device that's worked for me (with one canine waiting in my driveway, not three) is sugar hypnosis. When my landlady is not about, I throw the cur cookies from the car window before daring to disembark.

The All and the Void

A broadside in *Santa Fe Sun* cautions us to differentiate opinion from truth. So I must caution the reader that what follows is mere opinion. As I read in the parental *Sun:* The truth is, was, and always will be; the truth is not your opinion even if you're right.[3]

To put it another way, can a workaholic become a *dharma* bum? Can a self-inquisitor, a Dostoyevskian if earthbound Taurean, ever reach Nirvana?

Ram Dass assures us that the *bodhisattvas* have renounced Nirvana until every sentient being on earth gets there. Later, however, he issues a yawning disclaimer: Forget meditation, Sufi dancing, mind control seminars, and actualizations. This possibility will never come to pass because of the worldly power of inertia. Ferguson agrees that transformation is a journey with no final destination. As for stress, you can only win races by taking your foot off the accelerator. But do not despair, saith Sufi poet Rumi, for no ripe grape becomes sour.

The Solution According to Ram Dass

The way to Nirvana, in the words of Ram Dass, is through a radical change in our body cells brought about by a radical change in consciousness. In the process, we become avatars. But it isn't that easy. Contrary to New Age belief, we have to descend in order to ascend, we have to participate in "a descent of the greater whole polarizing the

ascent of individuals open to larger horizons of reality."⁴ No psychedelic
drugs for tuning out. No ducking into spaceships or UFOs.

Jesus Gets Around

Suppose writers of the New Testament reappeared to face the exegesis of
centuries? They might not have trouble with the now popular *Aquarian
Gospel of Jesus the Christ*. Transcribed from the Akashic Records by Levi,
born in 1844 in Belleville, Ohio, this book purports to be "The Philosophic
and Practical Basis of the Religion of the Aquarian Age of the World."

Presumed to be Christian, Levi wrote of the life and works of Jesus in
Tibet, India, Persia, Assyria, Greece, and Egypt, as well as the education of
Mary and Elizabeth in Zoan. In Orissa (India), the Day Star Jesus is welcomed
by Brahmanic priests who teach him the Vedas and the Manic laws. In
Greece, he is met by Apollo and addresses Athenians in the amphitheater.

The text introduces astrology in the person of Abraham, father of the
Jewish race, who taught the science of the stars, while in Persia the sun
god Ahura Mazda was worshipped, according to Zarathustra. In this
sacred mishmash, Elihu teaches the Buddhist doctrine, and the lessons of
Salome include the Chinese Tao!

Jesus even visits the Lhasa temple in Tibet with Vidyapati, an Indian
guide, and confers with Mengtse over ancient manuscripts. In short, Jesus
is a miracle-performing globe-trotter who brings together all the wisdom
of ancient religions under an Aquarian umbrella.

A New Age

The Aquarian Age, from Levi's perspective, was to be the era of the Son
of Man, an age of wisdom and spirituality to replace the warlike Piscean
period. As he put it, "In Spirit I was caught away into the realms of
Akasha; I stood alone within the circle of the sun."⁵ Here Aquarian
seraphim and cherubim proclaim the gospel of the Aquarian Age, where-
in the quest *is* the transformation.

Perhaps the transformation is of the unapologetic self.

Chapter Two

The Flower Children Come into Age

Boomers and Bloopers

It is estimated that the mean age of New Agers is forty-eight (which places them squarely with the baby boomers) and that the majority are women. According to the American Society for Retired Persons, seniors (defined as those fifty-five and older), are now the most populous and powerful lobby group in the United States. Power aside, the gap between the boomers and the bloopers is only seven years! One boomer has suggested that alternative society is composed of "complementary catalysts or centers of light." Sounds good. Most agree that New Age means an alternative lifestyle that may include communal living in "intentional communities." Hardly a new idea.

At least one communal model could potentially restore the word *senile* to our vocabulary. It calls itself the "Child's Garden . . . For the Children Inside Us All." On the other side are models built on global responsibility that embrace peacemaking and ecological agendas. Such groups talk—as do those working with death—about spiritual growth, enlightenment, light, and love. Their leaders are hip yogis focused on the "evolution of consciousness." One such group boasts an Italian princess, a stewardess, and a Zulu chieftain.

What's in a Name?

High Wind, Heartlight Morning Star, Linden Grove, Mountain Grove, Rainbow Ridge, and The Farm emphasize harmony with nature and self. My favorite community name is Truth Consciousness—which may or may not, according to its leader, Pujya Swamiji, lead to a life attuned with the divine. This group is commendably media-conscious, producing books, tapes, and a calendar.

A group in Los Angeles is even more ambitious: their goal is "transformation of the planet." Will they eliminate animal, vegetable, or mineral? They have no plans to exile technology. Curiously, the Center for Psychological Revolution has metamorphosed into the Center for the Examined Life. My prize for the most unpronounceable name goes to the New Hrsikesa Foundation, followers of Bhakti yoga. They abhor meat and "illicit" sex.

For Those with Special Needs

If you are looking for a communal lifestyle designed "for womyn only," try Pagoda/Crow's Nest, a metaphorical mélange. On Shaker land rests the Sufi Abode of the Message. What is the message? The Abode describes itself as an experiment with a shooting range. I don't think that Women's Land of Oregon offers this provision, although it frowns on owners and tenants. Agape Community is not a nudist colony but a Russian Orthodox enclave. The Gesundheit Institute used to treat sneezers and nonsneezers by delivering health care, straight and otherwise, until it opened a "dream hospital."

I haven't yet come across any exclusively senior arrangements, but just wait. These people are all getting older. Besides, such high-aiming folks don't aim to discriminate. Longer living seniors existing in this critical historic moment have become an ecological necessity—especially those who insist on seeking out an organic or socially relevant Garden of Eden. Perhaps that's what is meant by "going beyond survival."

Hag versus Sage

As the Christian church hunted witches to burn and to bake, as the Islamic world hunted down Arab queens and ancient Hebrew Shekinas who embodied the curse of death, so is today's postmenopausal woman regarded as the Mala Fortuna, the doomsayer and evil eye. Whereas an elder male is seen to embody a sage whose every wrinkle is revered, an elder female is the butt of jokes. She is the witch and the proverbial mother-in-law, the one whose procreative force is diseased. Abyssinian Christians swore that Jesus had decreed the hag's death by burning and the scattering of her ashes to prohibit resurrection. To date, some of the swearing continues.

At the twilight of the gods sits the northern goddess Skadi who, like the Dravidian goddess Kali, the formless one, became a black shadow that ate all the deities. She is the *vagina dentata,* or bottomless hole, into which even deified phalluses are sucked, fulfilling the creator Mother's curse as she devours what she brought forth.

The Hysterical Hysterectomy

At the pubescent age of forty, as I questioned a recommended hysterectomy and loss of my womb, my physician asked, "What do you need it for?" Eventually, I rejected the surgery, based as it was on throwing away a vital part of my womanly identity. The inference was that at forty, my biological destiny—my only value as a human breeding machine—was passé and that the mere possession of a womb at my age was obscene.

Had I questioned a male authority figure during the Renaissance, I could have been convicted of "scolding," been put in an iron bridle, and had spikes driven through my cheeks or tongue. Instead, I wrote poems about the "hysterical hysterectomy" and the patriarchal knife that offered to relieve me of proof of my gender.

Transformations

History reveals women's magical powers of transformation. Sarah, "the Queen," conceived and bore her child at the ripe crone age of ninety.[1] Elizabeth conceived John the Baptist in her old age.[2] Such details show that patriarchal writers thought "the inner wise blood of postmenopausal women could still perform its regenerative miracle."[3]

Recently, however, Americans let loose as much horror as amazement upon learning that an elderly woman, lying about her true age to receive artificial insemination, had borne a child for a daughter-in-law who could not. Is this, we wondered, an example of Margaret Mead's "postmenopausal zest"?

Old age in women is not only ugly but sinful, whereas in men it is distinguished. Why else would so many more women than men submit to the knife to be sliced up like lunch meat?

The Gleam of Homeless Hags

Other aging Ophelias and Violettas wandering city streets have a New Age gleam in their eyes. While these Ophelias do not wait to be bricked in, the dancing Violettas are arthritics at an opera ball. If the metal baskets they drag are not golden coaches, they carry no mortgages. If their ball gowns are tattered, the balloons flattened into old-lady boobs, their eyes gleam like cobwebbed chandeliers.

These homeless hags fancy themselves free of nagging children and wet-diapered grandkids. No more stinky cigars smelling up the parlor. No more babysitting for squalling brats. No more gritty dishes in the sink. No more leaking toilets and dripping faucets.

Who Yearns for Rose Corsages Anymore?

If the mirrors are smoked and cracked, who's looking? If the flower-children baby boomers are fat cats with two-car garages and lots of unpaid plastic cards, who's crying? The "new" flower children—those untabulated, off the census, and on the streets—look as old as Methusaleh.

Other Methusalehian posies perch high on their pensions, their Keoghs and IRAs, group tours, and church bingo games. Encapsulated in their condos, cottages, capital gains, or wheelchairs, they are glued to TV's CNN and the budget debates, stuck in vases of stagnant water, losing their petals one by one.

Where have all the flowers gone? Gone to peat moss, every one.

Chapter Three

Edgar, Deepak, Marianne, and Shirley

Healers at Heaven's Gate

In the Beginning

Before there was a firmament in the midst of the New Age waters, there was Edgar Cayce, a currently revered early-twentieth-century psychic who gave more than 14,000 "readings" in a state of altered consciousness. Flat on his back, like a woman preparing to be delivered of a child, the seer of seers spoke out in biblical syntax. The whole answer to the world, he declared, is to "love thy Lord, thy God, with all thy heart, and thy neighbor as thyself."[1] As each person sets this law into action, so will the little acts of love "leaven the whole lump."

Does this information sound new? Its effect over the past forty years has been revolutionary, to say nothing of its impact over the two thousand years since it was first recorded. Jesus did not call this law soul development; nor did he diagram funnels of leveled consciousness encompassing the cerebrospinal and autonomic nervous systems topped by the highest spiritual or superconsciousness tier. Jesus forgot the endocrine glands through which the Kundalini forces are summoned. Perhaps he was not told by God the Father: The glands are storehouses of cosmic memory. Put that in your begging bowl and drink it. Then stir in Cayce's proclamation that the soul is "God's companion."[2]

The Power of High Colonics

Who could resist Cayce's healing powers, illuminated as they were by Old Testament twitches of Mark, John, and Matthew—archetypes of the collective unconscious—and reanimated by high colonics at regular intervals? His recipe for body massage directed that peanut and olive oils be mixed with dissolved lanolin and rose water. Viewing the body as the temple of God, he recommended diet, exercise, and osteopathic adjustments to further lubricate the fountain of youth. Adjust the spine! Improve blood circulation! Go with the flow!

The New Age demands that we all take responsibility for our own health—especially for hormones, those biochemical terrorists dispatched by the glands. The seven eyes of the Lamb will open the Seven Seals, or *chakras,* functions of the divine spirit. God has stripped down to his *dhoti.*

Physician Emeritus

Enter Deepak Chopra, MD, director of the Shao Institute for Human Potential and Mind-Body Medicine. If Edgar was high priest of the New Age, Deepak is its physician emeritus.

His book *Journey into Healing,* subtitled *Awakening the Wisdom Within You,* is a clutch of postcard aphorisms embellished with third-eye graphics and borders. The flyleaf informs us that we are about to undergo "a transcendent experience." Not only will the words heal; they will alter our consciousness, bringing lasting peace and perfect health.

The text by this Ayurvedic practitioner cum physician veers between banality and obscurity. There's "The body is not a frozen sculpture. It is a river of information." Also "No matter how different they appear, body and mind are both soaked through with intelligence." And "The cosmic mind whispers to us . . ."[3]

Tiptoe through the Daisies

Having hung out his MD shingle, Deepak has much to say about health, pain, and disease. "If I find a green meadow splashed with daisies and sit down by a clear-running brook," he tells us, "I have found medicine."[4] He may also have found poison ivy, nettles, stinging bees, and sneezy allergies. Fear, however, is ill-advised, for "so long as the flow of change within us is fresh, we will be perfectly healthy."[5]

It's all so easy that Dr. Chopra, sowing Vedic panaceas, has also given us the book *Creating Health,* almost sinisterly subtitled *Beyond Prevention.* There's even *Creating Affluence.* As my mother used to say, good health is like money in the bank. With Vedic inspiration, we can splash—or smash—into "infinite reservoirs."

A Purveyor of Miracles

If Deepak is a sorcerer of survival, Marianne Williamson is a radiant Jew-healer in Christ clothing. Her disciples write letters to their AIDS or cancer, and behold, the diseases write back! What else can we expect from this purveyor of *A Course in Miracles*?

The *Course* workbook has a year's worth of daily lessons, although someone cheated (or had carpal tunnel syndrome) and lumped lessons 361 through 365 into one terse paragraph. This masterwork is the basis for Williamson's *A Return to Love.*

Whereas Deepak shuttles between health and illness, Marianne trips on love, not fear. Her personal confessions convince us that she is sincere as well as gifted. Like Deepak, she is strong on "miraculous change." If he is Rama and Pan, she is Gaia, handmaiden to the crucified Jesus, breathless for resurrection. In her Pietà, unlike Michelangelo's, she surrenders—if not sags—to her man, despite repetitive setbacks.

But then we are told, "The love of God is the love of everyone."[6] New Age seeress, Marianne's precepts are traditional Christian litanies: "I am as God created me" ("I'm okay; you're okay") and "Pray, pray and pray."[7]

Have you found anything new here? Certainly not the swooning of the "instrument," the ecstatic kneeling to prayer, the appeal for the miracle, which arrives on time like a FedEx delivery. Religion and psychotherapy marry. When your knees give out, meditate.

Ego, Go Away!

Is the meaning of New Age that the ego must vacate us so that the Old Age Holy Spirit might move in? Spirit's job, it seems, is to reveal our function and then help us forget it. Free will has surrendered. According to Edgar, will is merely an aspect of soul, God's companion.

Marianne in her patchwork dress bedazzles God the Prince. Like Edgar and Deepak, she swears that everyone can be successful. "Disease is loveless thinking," she admonishes.[8] Peace will come from change. We're "all perfect"—or at least we were until the Fall.

If we're perfect, why this haranguing to change? If we can simply stretch out our hand to heaven, why work so hard to transform?

Love . . . inner peace . . . surrender to a divinity. What's new here—the goal or the means? Lecturing at a psychic supermarket instead of a cathedral is new. Paradise lost is perfect health. While Deepak asserts that perfect health takes no work, *A Course in Miracles* is exhausting in size and depth. Unlike God's plan for the universe, it leaves no seventh day for rest.

Who Can We Blame?

From where does New Age emanate? From imported doctrines—those of Moses, Jesus, Buddha, Lao-tzu, the sutras—incorporated into models of Karma and grace espoused by proselytizers, speakers in tongues, and greeting-card vendors. From the myth that the world is sick. Yet if it is sick, so are we. At this point, Old Age seems preferable. If we are dying, we can still have a hell of a good time. Even Deepak admits, "No one has ever found a new world by worrying about it."[9]

A doctor from India shrugged and said to me, as my mother lay dying, "Why are you crying? Your mother is only one mote in the universe." I confess, now as then, it is hard to see my mother, dying from gangrene contracted in a major city hospital, as just one more of Deepak's "stagnant pools washed clean by the tide." Or as a failure of Marianne's attitudinal healing. Was gangrene to be averted through inner peace? In The World According to Edgar, Deepak, and Marianne, the reply is a resounding *yes!*

Hoofing Spirit Consciousness

Shirley MacLaine agrees. In the view of this former hoofer and Sinatra rat pack ecstatic of Hollywood, Peru, the Himalayas, and Santa Fe, her mother's repeated bone fractures were the old lady's own fault. This archetype of determinism is stated in New Age psychobabble as "You make your own reality." Having forsaken the law of love, the notion that body and spirit are one, our hormonal messages have become garbled. We self-produce cancer, failed love affairs and marriages, as well as osteomyelitis.

Lest this interpretation of altered (higher?) consciousness appears mean-spirited, MacLaine hoofs us back to her origins. In a shed in Santa Fe, to which she returns repeatedly, she records her journeys through past lives, pausing only to practice yoga, chant mantras, and take apple cider vinegar baths to clear the toxins.

The Pricks of Quantum Physics

Shirley adopts Cayce's Christ-centered dictum that human illness derives from sin. For her, illness comes from a split personality: good versus evil. God, on the other hand, is one. And with oneness there can be no evil. Duality is therefore unacceptable.

Shirley's obsession with illness as an imbalance of forces rotating about the atoms of our bodies seems to derive more from Cayce than from her readings in quantum physics. Is she being simplistic?

We know by now that Edgar didn't invent the material he imparted. It can be traced back to writing from East Indian and Chinese ancients, as well as Christian sources, that urged humans to tune into cosmic universal consciousness. From the Sanskrit, Like begets like. Karma implies that we must work out in this lifetime what we did not resolve in past lives. Western use of the word *Karma* brings forth an image of a roulette wheel containing all our alleged incarnations.

Shlepping through Karma

My mother's word for carrying such a heavy load through eternity was *shlepping,* "Why are you *shlepping* all that stuff around?" she'd ask. "Are

you a *meshuginah* (nut)?" Like any mother—Jewish, Christian, or atheist—she would urge me to sit down and take the load off my feet. To
work out all the "required" details with her before she left, would I have
had to rediscover her as a Mesopotamian peddler, an Egyptian belly
dancer, a Nubian slave trader, a cat or bat or *Tyrannosaurus rex?*

Suppose she were a hoofer, an actress, a writer, a mystic, and a
cveching daughter all in one lifetime? Where would I start—or stop? Take
it from a senior, who now and then would like a little peace. Isn't it easier to pop a dose of Tylenol sitting up than to lie down and let a stranger
make a pincushion out of you?

New Age Not Only Hurts, It's Too Much Work

Edgar's parameters were time, space, and . . . patience! Shirley's are limitless.

Visualize her through quivering acupuncture needles placed strategi-
cally in her forehead (third eye), throat, ears, and belly, as she appears
in everything from her Academy Award–winning acting performance,
one-woman Broadway and Vegas shows, and bestselling author confes-
sionals to her previous lives as a nun with scuffed shoes, a pirate with a
peg leg, a Buddhist monk, and in a Kiplingesque vision, as Asana, "leg-
endary" princess of the elephants who could communicate from hundreds of miles distant. If you dare go further, see her in her penultimate
incarnation—which she admits is outrageous—as a founder of the new
Spiritual Republic of the United States, along with the writers of the
Constitution and Declaration of Independence!

How to Respond

If you have questions about healing, don't ask me and don't write to
Shirley. She gets too much fan mail already. You could try channeling
Edgar Cayce. Or waiting by a clear-running brook in a TV commercial;
who knows, Deepak just might amble along carrying a calf for a
caduceus while Marianne skips by murmuring to the brook, "Pray, pray,
pray." You could also—and this is really far out—try ordering a book
called *Sexual Encounters with Extraterrestrials.* If none of these options
work, dial a psychic!

Chapter Four

Tripping the Paranormal

If I Go So Far Out, How Do I Get Back?

Is Old Age Normal?

To many of those who are younger, age looks paranormal, defined by the *Oxford English Dictionary* as "beyond the scope of normal objective investigation or explanation." To the young, seniors appear weird. We might as well have descended from spaceships like one-eyed dwarf ghouls.

Youths shudder. They'll never look like us. When they're not blackmailed to act respectfully, they clearly despise us—the mirror of what they might, God forbid, become. At less than sixty years of age, while in a parking lot near-collision, I was thrown the epithet "You're *old*." Although I wasn't driving, I was instantly shrunk like a skull on a pole. Incidents like this explain why, when we stick to shuffleboard or needlepoint, we're drawn so far out.

Remember the 1960s

Remember when Timothy Leary seemed pretty far gone? So easy was it at thirty-plus to look askance at those wild flower-children cavorting on

Berkeley's Elysian Fields. Who would have thought that by the time I got to sixty, those who had lasted would be tripping not just locally and globally, but intergalactically? And that the engine driving us would be "experience enhancement"?

Psychic phenomena—known cozily to the *cognoscenti* as psi—now comprise the mystery dimension. The list of New Age voyages includes such attractions as intergalactic travel, out-of-body events, clairvoyance (seeing from a distance), telepathy, life after death (reincarnation) and near-death experiences, psychokinesis (interaction of mind and matter) and psychosurgery, synchronicity, astral travel, precognition, channeling, healing crystals, levitation, dowsing, auras, ghosts, and plant consciousness. But how do consciousness and the material world interact?

Of Course, There's Déjà Vu

Déjà vu refers to that which has been already seen. Have I been here before? Did the image come from a movie I saw as a child or from indigestion? In this category the list of paranormal phenomena expands (in alphabetical order) into alien abductions, Bigfoot, biorhythms, fortune telling, Loch Ness monster, moon madness, Ouija boards, past-life therapy, phrenology, psychometry, pyramid power, seances, spontaneous human combustion (does this mean *love?*), and table tipping (the table tips, not the client).

The Supernatural Is Awesome

Interest in astrology has grown by leaps and bounds. According to *Life Magazine,* the number of astrologers has quintupled from 1,000 to 5,000. Forty-eight percent of the American population says that astrology may be or is valid. The metaphysical is physical. Most of us doubted that a nightclub magician could bend a steel spoon by mind power alone until Uri Geller mystified psychologists at the Stanford Research Center.

Since the 1968 publication of Linda Goodman's *Sun Signs,* annual sales of books on the subject have reached 20 million. We procure individual chart readings for anywhere between fifty and two hundred dollars, seeking to know what part of the zodiac the sun was traveling through at the moment of our birth.

Harmonic Convergence As an Urge

To revive occult beliefs, we stand under trees at midnight, or checking our watches, drum pulses on sand dunes to establish harmonic convergence with millions around the world. Crystals around our necks clarify the radiance of the millennial dawn. We hover about black-clothed tables to make contact with spirit entities of the fourth, fifth, or even seventh dimension. We talk to our plants, and rush to psychic fairs to cleanse our auras.

Is the Bermuda Triangle a hoax? Has the government been lying about the UFOs at Roswell? You'd never know it from the fifty-year celebrations planned there the week of the dummies' landing. The government swears they were demo dummies, and not aliens. Even if they were aliens, they must have been dummies to bypass glitzy Las Vegas in order to land in godforsaken Roswell, where there wasn't any there *there* until their arrival.

Does ESP Stand for Even Sex Maniacs Pretend (Orgasm)?

A senior calls a friend who says, "I've just been thinking about you." That proves that there's ESP. With Peter Fonda and Audrey Hepburn gone, she cannot settle quietly by Golden Pond. She has her palm read. She tries tuning into the channel of one who's channeling. Just wait down there—silently— until she finishes levitating. No hurry. It feels too good to come down.

If she cannot run a marathon, how will the endorphins kick in? As for AARP diehards who have signed up for long-distance running in Boston or New York or Timbuktu, I don't want to hear from you until I finish my slow turtle laps around the pool.

Knock Knock, Who's There?

If there is other intelligent life in the universe, its aptitude starts with those of us who have been around the block more than once. We're stones that kick off moss, or dissolve moss in raspberry vinaigrette. Did you know that a "vinaigrette" was once a bottle used for smelling salts?

In earlier times we seniors were known for our faints. Lady seniors wore corsets, stockings with garters, and longline brassieres. We were assumed to vote Republican, to be Conservative on issues of foreign and domestic debt, down on taxes and on spending. Later, they would call us Reds, Communists of the Evil Empire. Now, we vote Green.

President Bush—Meet Tiresias

Tell me, what is former President Bush doing with his finger on the chute release? Parachute gate may be a test for impotence or a plot to make contact with a UFO. The CIA has been infiltrated by New Age ideas.

Like blind Tiresias, Bush's peers are walking beaches, tapping long sticks into the berm to find water. Water, said Lao-tzu, "is the weakest and softest of things, yet overcomes the strongest and hardest." Water, like the soul, is everlasting. Which is why, in our crepuscular years, we're still searching for the Fountain of Youth.

That Witch Is a Spirit Channeler

Others of us study precognition and telepathy. The Old Age version of both was Mother's *I told you so. I told you you'd go off a cliff.* (We did, with her voice in our ear.) *I told you if you went in the ocean you'd drown.* (Which is why we denied that we nearly did.) *I told you you'd fall off that bike.* (Mom, we didn't see the hill.) In olden times, our moms would have been burned at the stake. Which is why we called old women witches. Now we call them spirit guides or channelers.

Dibbyk . . . or Dirty Old Man

Old women—and men—can now safely welcome demonic possession (a last-call pregnancy) and not be carted off to the pyre. A friend tells about a *dibbyk*like spirit who penetrated a roommate. The victim, a down-to-earth nurse, refused to admit to the *dibbyk*'s existence. Nevertheless, every few days her language would devolve into gutturals. My friend tried to exorcise the demon. She accused the nurse of allowing the house poltergeists to inhabit her without protest.

The estate did appear to be haunted. Its former owner, a famous folksinger, had never liked to stay there. My friend was convinced that before her own tenure began, the poltergeists had dug in. She implored the Catholic Church for a formal exorcism. Had they seen the shop in town that specialized in gear for satanic rites?

Although the Church complied, the house was so ghost-ridden that a future there appeared hopeless. Doors slammed behind the occupants; they felt the unseen pull on them, causing them to fall or objects to fall upon them.

Were the troublemakers astral spirits, household familiars, ghosts in animal or fiery form, these knockers who made mysterious noises? Were they "fetches, doppel-gangers . . . wraiths of the sick, the dying and the newly dead"?[1] The dead, it seemed, had returned to seek revenge, or merely human company. In fear for their lives the remaining pair (who had succeeded in ridding the premises of the possessed one) quitted the place themselves.

Wraiths and Other Disturbers

Gillian Bennett divides such supernatural disturbers into the good and bad dead. The good dead include wraiths, fetches, and warning ghosts. These are defended as benevolent family spirits who return to reassure, warn, or assist us. Poltergeists and hauntings are brought by the evil dead, who are disruptive and malevolent. I'm still trying to fit in the bogeyman, who has nothing to do with picking your nose. Was the bogeyman a fetch? We were told he'd come to fetch us if we didn't eat our peas.

According to a sixteenth-century writer, such restless souls will "upset furniture, bastinado, nip, thump and bastoon persons, throwing stones and tiles at them, holding doors and jamming them. . . . endamaging property and perilously molesting men and women."[2]

Are the possessed hysterics to be treated by psychotherapy or as candidates for exorcism? When belief in diabolic possession ebbed in the nineteenth century, there arose a belief in possession by evil departed or discarnate souls who sought lodging. The Lord's Prayer still beseeches God to release us from evil.

Author Aldous Huxley was on the side of the devils. "If the evidence for clairvoyance, telepathy and prevision is accepted," he wrote, "then we must allow that there are mental processes which are largely independent of space, time and matter."[3]

Witches Were Universal Scapegoats

During centuries of persecution, witches—most commonly, old poor women—became scapegoats for all that went wrong with humans: dry wells and failed crops, lightning and fire, and the alleged demonic possession of children. "The witch-hunting mania gave men an excuse for their own faults and failures," says Barbara Walker. It was convenient for getting rid of unwanted, poor, solitary or nonfertile females; contentious wives; rebellious daughters; shrewish neighbors. It made money for the churches. It allowed sexually starved men to sublimate their repressions in the form of sadism."[4]

If old women healers, priestess descendants of the wise goddess, cured without a university decree, the church proclaimed them witches to be burnt at the stake after torture designed to coerce confession. They were especially singled out for aiding women to give birth safely and less painfully. As Walker informs us, "In the sixteenth century Scottish church-wardens were ordered to report to the authority any such obstetrical 'charms, sorceries, enchantments, invocations,' and other such witch-crafts as the classical priestesses used."[5]

Where Are They Now?

Were the melancholy and the chronic headaches I suffered from suscep-tible to exorcism? If so, I might have saved myself thousands of dollars in therapy and Valium. The Valium was replaced not by witch spells, whale fetus, shark stomach, liver pills, or powdered rhinoceros horn, but by swimming and writing. If devils (including the famished dead) inhab-ited my flesh, they did quit, unable to subsist on H_2O and daily odes.

Hungry Ghosts

The Japanese in Kyoto light fires on the mountain to guide hungry ghosts to annual feasts laid out to appease them. New Age believers hire cre-ative channelers to make contact with the dead, as well as with their own spirits of higher consciousness. Prodded by needles, Shirley MacLaine's sibyl revealed herself as a svelte seven-foot giant ready to fix on tape the mysteries of the cosmos. In folklore wraiths are a commonplace of oral tradition. They may be a sign of one's own impending death, harbinger of a family member passing, a calamity omen.

Other antiquarian omens include screech owls or three knocks at the head of a bed, a bleeding nose, rats gnawing at window or bed hangings, or the breaking of a looking glass. Jews cover all house mirrors after a death in the family.

Satan and Evil

For centuries Christian churches have been wrestling with the problem of evil. Exorcisers and priests have sent many people to the stake and public condemnation. Satan was an angel who, like Lucifer, alienated himself from God. Huxley called him the Chief Executive of a tribe of troublesome devils that include "the *haute bourgeoisie*" of hell. A seventeenth-century theologian spoke of nonmalignant spirits that include "fauns, nymphs and satyrs of the ancients, the hobgoblins of the European peasantry, the poltergeists of modern psychical researchers."[6] Incubi and succubi were as prevalent as ants.

Huxley deplored the raising of Satan to God status, allowing the obsession with eradicating evil to triumph over celebrating the good. "By thinking primarily of evil we tend, no matter how excellent our intentions, to create opportunities for evil to manifest itself."[7]

Shakespeare Is Still Alive

ESP is not the exclusive property of New Agers. Old Agers, as well, have long claimed experience in denial of the paranormal. If Shakespeare be believed, Caesar's assassination was preceded by omens and unheeded warnings.

Palmistry—the future seen not in a grain of sand, but in the landscape of the hand—may be solicited to keep a step ahead of one's doom. Incense sticks may be lit to cleanse the house. Mantras or sacred spells can be recited. We may be inspired by the Beatles' trip to an East Indian guru, or Allen Ginsberg's *ohms* to marijuana crowds, or Deepak Chopra's mass hypnosis on TV. Ancient precedents are revealed on Nile papyrus, on Aztec and Mesopotamian tablets, on Chinese and Palestinian scrolls, and in ancient Vedic texts, as well as in the Egyptian and Tibetan Books of the Dead.

Does Out of Body Mean Out of Mind?

Out-of-body events should be welcomed with hallelujahs. What senior does not confront in the mirror glass, like Dorian Gray, the wraith of her impending end? In twenty years we have put on forty pounds. Our faces have caved in to landslides. How can we think straight when we ourselves are tilted? What happened to the North and South Poles? Breasts and rear ends fall in like Jell-O molds. If only we could get out of these out-of-shape bodies and try on others like new clothes. Which may be why the penultimate and purifying white light of death can look so appealing.

Psychosurgery, Hallucinogens, and Horoscopes

If we turn back from death, pleading that our children need us, why not try psychosurgery—a painless, knifeless reshaping? I'd say, go for it. (And in sparing the knife, be sure to ask for the discount.) No wonder we are apt to grasp at passing poltergeists, animal, vegetable, or mineral, or deny The End with dreams of a promising new incarnation. (Are pre-cognitive dreams chance reshapings of recent events?) The dread of the expected is revealed in the saying Forewarned is forearmed.

For seniors hallucinogens went out a generation ago. We've had it up to here with medically prescribed drugs. Besides, we have enough memories to last out our lifetimes. The future's a different story. What skeptic doesn't cheat with an occasional peek at their daily newspaper horoscope? How many stars guide us today? Journalist gurus allow us three to five apiece.

Astrology is a mariner guided by celestial bodies. I was recently reminded that its effects do not start and stop with its alleged influence on human affairs. Through astrological vigilance, an acquaintance my age, mixing heraldic symbols for earth, air, and water, hopes to breed both the perfect horse and a live revival of the mythical unicorn, complete with deer feet, goat beard, and lion tail.

Senile Goes Kaput

Within the scope of paranormalcy, senile behaviors are acceptable. The term "senile," however, has been replaced by "age-challenged." In the twilight zone, I can leave my body as often as I want, provided that I have a safe landing place. I can screech like a monkey or cluck like a hen, and still be welcome in the local chorus. Such behavior is called New Age, not "eccentric." When did "eccentric" lose "whimsical" and "capricious"? When did "eccentric" become "old"?

Seniors are induced to dive off into deep water when we sat for generations dipping our ankles in pools. We leap helter-skelter off cliffs on guy ropes: *Look, Ma, I'm dancing!* We soar in gliders and climb rocks to kingdom come.

We're living longer and we've never been in better shape. We wait in snowdrifts for a rendezvous with extraterrestrials in a flying saucer, fantasizing scenes of hostage-taking by one-eyed ghouls. I thought that stuff went out with *Perils of Pauline* and the sexy hirsute abductor King Kong.

We Intend to Live until You're Sick of Us

If drugs are not the engine that drives us as they did Leary's kids, what is? Proving our self-worth as age strives to diminish it, or simply not giving a damn, since we're running out of time? At sixty, even fifty and above, we have the right to a near-death experience. I may want to make sure there is life after death before saying yes when my guide arrives. I think I should taste each item in the buffet before overdosing on the wrong choice.

Choice at Ninety

Choice is no more radical at ninety than choosing to give birth. Radical, because we did not choose to be born. In New Age parlance, we "create our own reality." This senior rallying cry is the refusal of old dogs to lie down. Instead of shaking our fists at the Lethean guide, we ought to invite her in for a cup of herbal tea that we might not live to finish.

Speaking of choice at ninety, the eighty-nine-year-old mother of a friend of mine received a questionnaire on birth control. She wrote back, "My name isn't Biblical Sarah."

While in a semicoma after surgery, my mother described her out-of-body experience. She was in the dark tunnel, floating above her own shell on the hospital bed, when Grandpa appeared and beckoned, *Come*. What did Mother do? What she always did in flashes of clairvoyance. She said, "This is ridiculous" and returned to live one more decade.

Mother Hadn't Heard of Precognition

My mother would have scoffed at ESP. She had never read the works of Dr. Elisabeth Kübler-Ross, but she knew trouble when she saw it. At the age of eighty, she treated death like she did her younger brother's offer to come sit with her on New Year's Eve: "Who needs them? They're boring. All we'll do is watch TV. I'd rather play mah-jong with the girls."

Mother didn't believe in life after death; she would sooner cash in her chips now. Nor did she leave The Neighborhood. My generation thinks differently. If the world is our oyster, we stretch to touch the pearl—even if it beckons from a spaceship.

Chapter Five

Is Holism Hokey . . .
or History?

Wholly Holy Holy

Does it bother you as much as me that holistic has come to mean holy? The word is infallible as the Virgin's virginity, not only a tautology but an open sesame to instant credibility.

Holistic derives from *kalos,* a Greek root from which stems *health, whole,* and *holy.* Medically, holism entails treating the whole person, including mental and social factors, rather than just the symptoms of a disease.

Holism views the source of illness as a disturbance in the life force. It looks back to Asian, Ayurvedic (East Indian), and Hippocratic traditions of empirical healing that stress human balance with the environment. Holism also admits to links with pagan Gnosticism, ancient astronomy, astrology, alchemy, magic, and ecstatic practices. It subscribes to faith in the body's self-healing properties.

Interventions

Holistic therapies include physical interventions such as acupuncture and acupressure, diet and chemistry (herbology, polarity and neuropathy, fasting and vitamin chemistry), energetic modalities (homeopathy, psychic healing, innovative psychology), and self-exercise therapies, referred to as bodywork (yoga, Alexander technique, Rolfing, aerobics, Tai Chi, dance therapy, and polar energetics). Innovative psychology—usually referred to as stress reduction—embraces meditation, hypnosis, self-hypnosis, and guided visualizations. These methods are also spoken of as theurgic ritual exercises capable of elevating the soul.

Facing the Facts

What's in a face? In holistic health, plenty. Physiognomy presents facial characteristics as clues to character as well as illness; for instance, narrow spacing between the eyes is supposed to signify low tolerance for or impatience with the passing of time. A chart breaks down the features into a grid that minutely links portions of the facial landscape with bodily organs and functions. Another term for this study, proposed by Robert Whiteside, is personology. If I accept the New Age belief in self-responsibility for disease, should I accuse my left nostril or right cheek of infamies?

Book Titles on Holistic Health

Book titles on holistic health include: *Health in the New Age; Holistic Interpretations of Autism; Holistic Medicine: From Stress to Optimum; Holistic Resource Management; Inner Balance: The Power of a Holistic. . . .* (the library computer screen swallowed the rest); *The Healer Within; Mind As Healer, Mind As Slayer; Universal Life Energy* (the word *universal,* like *spiritual,* is ubiquitous in New Age material); *A Holistic Art: Prescriptions for Nutritional Healing/Drug-Free Remedies Using Vitamins, Minerals, Herbs and Food Supplements; The Practice of Aroma Therapy; The Woman's Holistic Headache Relief Book;* and *The New Natural Cat.*

Holistic Resource Management's chapter titles are equally bewildering. There's "The Time Dimension in Soil, Plant and Animal Relationships," for instance, and "Brittle and Non-Brittle Environments" (Glass Houses versus Wigwams?).

The Cure As Disease

Holism is so pervasive that I am often tempted to call the cure the disease. Cure implies an analytical approach—a breaking down and separation belied by the term. Remember the song about the bones: The thigh bone's connected to . . . The next bone's connected to . . . ? In personifying our individual body parts it becomes easy to treat the self as a dysfunctional kidney or a runaway heart. This way of thinking reminds me of Japanese dramas in which all action centers on the search for a long-lost child. What happened to my other bladder? Oh, I forgot; there's only one.

Holism *Is* about Wholeness

Wholeness is the antithesis of separation. From this perspective, dis-ease implies a lack of harmony, a refusal to change, to take Reichian self-responsibility for our élan vital, to manipulate our energy through appropriate channels. Holism advises us to concentrate on prevention, not pathology. Holism reminds me of Cayce's lump that's supposed to leaven the mass. Unfortunately, my mentality is cancer prone.

In *Health for the Whole Person* by Arthur C. Hastings, PhD, James Fadiman, PhD, and James S. Gordon, MD, we are told that the holistic approach to medicine and health "synthesizes the ecological sensitivity of ancient healing traditions and the precision of modern science," as well as "our personal concern with personal responsibility and spiritual and emotional growth, and our urge to democratic cooperation and social and political activism."[1] How much more whole can we get?

Hahnemann, Holistic Papa

Samuel Hahnemann is recognized as the father of the holistic, or empirical, approach to healing. His offspring is commonly referred to as homeopathic medicine, which utilizes minute doses of a substance to produce symptoms similar to those spawned by the ailment. In other words, like goes to like. Ancient Asians, too, observed that flowing with the opponent brings about gradual change. Spurred on by Hahnemann's followers, a grassroots herbalism was organized and refined. The spiritual essence of an herb was expected to work on the spiritual body.

Hahnemann's philosophic connection to Neoplatonism, which acknowledges the existence of soul, was not altogether endearing. Although joined by healers and health food advocates, he shocked opponents into founding in 1847 the American Medical Association (AMA).

Rationalist Medicine: What You See, You'll Get

Whereas holism does not isolate the disease from the diseased, traditional rationalist medicine does. The motto for this approach might be stated as *What you see, you'll get.*

Rationalist medicine, which began long before the founding of the AMA, is intent on seeking external causes for ailments and counteracting them by either balancing "humours" or injecting an antibiotic. Materialistic to the core, this discipline scoffs at the spiritual. Imagine mentioning spirit guides to your physician, or asking her to study your physiognomy or the eye's iris for signs of acute inflammation in the body, or to observe your forehead for indications of liver trouble. I suggest that you keep a stiff upper lip when asking your AMA practitioner to consult your meridian wheel. Don't expect her to check your lip to see how your stomach's doing.

Holism Does Not Scoff at Iridology

Holistic practitioners interest themselves in life events that occur in the setting where disease developed. A Social Readjustment Rating Scale from the *Journal of Psychosomatic Research* lists life events from the death of a spouse through jaywalking, and goes on to address therapeutic procedures and preventive measures. (Cross only at traffic signals?) The therapeutic procedures include reassurance, intravenous sodium amytal, and dream analysis.

Iridologists, like other New Age (from ancient) methodologists, believe that examining one part of the body reveals the whole. After observing features of the eye's iris—its lesions, rings, spots, and coloration—they prescribe cleansing diets, herbs, and exercise. So do not scoff at anyone who tells you, "I can see it in your eyes."

Nor is it a good idea to poke fun at a homeopath who wants to know if your symptoms intensify first thing in the morning, or on windy days. Although the principles of Hahnemann's discipline are scant, its practice requires acute observation of the effects of between one and two hundred commonly used remedies. Maladies are considered unique to the patient and, when treated, are apt to resolve, provided that the physician is skilled at memorization.

Ch'i

Chinese doctors practiced a system of holistic medicine 5,000 years ago. New Age or Old Age, it was based on a unified theory of energy imbalance that looked to cure *before* illness manifested. A primary cure was acupuncture, requiring the insertion of tiny needles to stimulate specific body points. Insertion points were determined by meridians (*ching*) or loci that were thought to control the functioning of internal organs. Chinese medicine focused on the vital energy, or *ch'i* (breath), of the body, which circulates along the acupuncture meridians. When the energy flow was blocked, one became susceptible to illness. Acupuncture stimulated the body's natural recuperative powers rather than introducing an external substance.

Since its inception Chinese medicine, like modern physics, has linked matter with energy. Men (and womyn) are viewed as reflections of a universe subject to the Tao, a divine law that requires us to live harmoniously with the forces in our world. Chief among them are the ebbing and flowing polarities known as *yin,* defined as negative or female, and *yang*, positive or male. Balance between the two, and between the *ch'i* and chakra energies, ensures good health for person and planet—a matrix for micro and macro.

We Add Psi to Ch'i

Not to be outdone by Easterners, holistic Western researchers have identified *psi,* whose forms include telepathy (mind-to-mind communication), clairvoyance (direct knowledge of objects and events, including disease conditions), precognition (awareness of future events), and psychokinesis (mental influence on matter, for such purposes as healing). Holistic practitioners experienced in these methods cannot forgive modern medics for isolating illnesses and attacking them directly. Indeed, we all know the dangers in this approach. Every substance introduced into the body has side effects of one sort or another. We say, "The cure is worse than the disease." We especially recoil from surgery.

What did healers use prior to the scalpel? A Greek mother I once knew walked about the house with leeches clinging to her affected parts; the house reeked of garlic. For years afterward I shunned the bulbous herb. Then someone told me that eating its cloves would cure the common cold. So the next time I came down with a sore throat and sniffles, I recuperated on garlic toast.

More on the Greeks

The empiricist-rationalist debate was born in Greece when Apollonians were exposed to ecstatic shamanism in Thrace and Scythia. Theatrical to the extreme, they couldn't help dabbling in out-of-body pranks, separation of the soul, and the pursuit of immortality, as well as spiritualist ideas in Orphism. Disdaining the material for the spiritual, they were influenced by the Lokayata school of India that debated the metaphysics of the elements, dropping *akasha* (ether) from the list of air, earth, water, and fire. These Indo-Iranian connections stressed wind as a life force. Even today we speak of losing our wind.

Trends in early naturalistic medicine continued with Origen, a third-century Greek physician and theologian who hinted at the preexistence of the soul. Transmigration of the soul, however, remained a dirty word to some Hellenists of the time, though not to Christian Gnostics, who believed in Buddhist and Hindu notions of rebirth. These radicals merged with Neoplatonists in staging trances and other Orphic rites throughout the Hellenistic world. In the fourth century, Orphists used Chaldean-Egyptian high magic to summon godlings.

The sixteenth century whisked in the prince of charlatans, Phillipus Aureolus Theophrastus Bombast von Hohenheim (1492–1541). Nicknamed Paracelsus, this empiricist attacked the rationalist "orthodox" church.

Referring to Aristotle, Galen, and Celsus as "so many high asses," Paracelsus practiced folk, even gypsy, medicine. He promised that the body, a valiant alchemist, would heal itself by balancing the *ch'i* and chakra energies.

The Traditionalists Had Not Been Asleep

All this time, traditionalists had stood up for rationalist Hippocratic medicine in the person of Avita Galen, a second-century Greek physician. Then naturalists took the veil. Empiricists, with their millennial visions, were forced into a counterculture of secret societies and decentralized networks that centuries later was to embrace several of our Founding Fathers. (Don't ask me for names.) There they awaited the Age of Aquarius, an inevitable follow-up to the Second Coming.

A Clean Sweep

Swept along with the early naturalists were Theosophist psychic healers: Gnostics, neo-Egyptian Rosicrucians, English Freemasons who dabbled in tarot and trance and Neoplatonic theurgy, spiritualist Swedenborgians of the New Jerusalem tripping through heaven and hell, Transcendentalists like Henry David Thoreau and Walt Whitman, Edgar Cayce, and Mary Baker Eddy, the priestess of Christian Science. Should we blame this clean sweep of empiricism on Western rationalists—especially sixth-century Pythagoras, father of them all—or on the East's trickster meridians? Should the slippery low-calorie trouts known as Sigmund Freud and Carl Jung, latecomers to the Last Supper, be allowed to slide off the hook?

In chasing down the Order of the Golden Dawn, does my evangelist itch, as Cayce would say, derive from the one true source of all empirical diseases—namely, putrefaction in the colon?

The Paradigm of Holistic Medicine

Neuroscientists and physicists have proposed theories to explain transcendental experiences, paranormal events, and perceptual oddities. Their hypotheses draw on theoretical mathematics and claim to incorporate the supernatural into nature. But is reality the product of an invisible matrix? Does sensory reality emerge, as Marilyn Ferguson suggests, "from a domain beyond time and space where only frequencies exist?"[2]

Other sources summarize the holistic approach to medicine as a synthesis of the "ecological sensitivity" displayed by ancient healing traditions and the "precision" of modern science. According to New Age thinking, illness expresses conflict, the body's response to stress, a body-mind connection. "A tumor is a process,"[3] we are told. We are advised, in another plea for integration, that even a rock is a dance of electrons. If this is true of a rock, then how can it not be true of the tumor? Defining a tumor as a process shifts the focus from the disease of an organ to its cause, and ultimately to its cure—which in a holographic universe is invariably personal transformation. Forging links of this sort is either an example of wishful thinking or, to the believer, a blessed savior.

What If the World Is a Hologram?

A hologram, in the words of my *Oxford English Dictionary,* is "a three-dimensional image formed by the interference of light beams from a coherent light force." Deepak Chopra's mind-body medicine, based on the premise that the world is a hologram, promises lasting peace with perfect health. Complete healing, he reminds us, depends on our capacity to stop struggling. Thus far I get it: go with the flow. But what am I to make of "lasting healing and lasting peace are real only at the level of our Being?"[4] I am awash in metaphysical mush!

Science has never been my strong suit. To conceive of modern physics wedded to lensless photography's three-dimensional images makes me dizzy, and dizziness breeds nausea. Even so, let's consider this marriage: lasers producing light waves that touch. Lyall Watson says that such light waves make interference patterns of light and dark ripples that can be reproduced on a photographic plate. One of the beams, instead of coming directly from the laser, reflects first off my face. You don't need 3–D glasses to see this hologram, this self-portrait of consciousness. To brain researchers, such a picture illustrates how we store memory.

Back to Wholeness

If a holographic image is broken, we are informed, any piece of it will reconstruct the entire image. Now, that's scary. Take out a piece of the lung, or an ovarian tumor, and pray that it will not regrow itself.

"Reality as illusion" sounds oddly similar to Gertrude Stein's "Is there *there?*" See Gertie the physicist, herself a holomovement. Picasso would be amused to hear his work described as a hologram, a mathematical transform.

Assuming the brain is a hologram representing the holographic universe, the blur must be all there is. And if the blur is reality, then the blurs I'm seeing are New Age lenscraft—or perhaps these old age eyes are dying. When I am told that light frequencies can transform the blurred potential into sound and color and touch and smell and taste, I can only shrug and say (to a physicist, not an optician, and never a rabbi), "Okay. If you think so, show me."

The Pursuit of Health Requires Me To Poke Holes in the Sacred

Years ago I bought a large costume-jewelry pendant in the shape of a cross. After its *faux* turquoise stone fell out, I would point to it and quip to my sister students, "This is my 'holey' cross." The only one who looked at me funny turned out to be a plainclothes nun.

It's not that the body-mind connection is not intrinsic to physical and mental health. Such a connection has been clear since Galen, that rationalist physician. It's just hard to apply the principles of critical thinking to the rolling back of eyes that occurs in response to questions about New Age, especially those greeted solemnly with the conversation stopper "It's holistic."

One thinker hints that we may be approaching the end of science, that Western civilization is moving into higher dimensions of human experience. Which is enough to give me a new ulcer.

The Ulcer Connection

Using past-life regression to previous incarnations may help me solve such mysteries as the sins I committed to make me prone to ulcers. An attitude table defines the duodenal ulcer sufferer as one who feels deprived of her due and wants to get even.

Let's try past-life regression: A camel kicked me in the chest. I was once a fire-eater. I swallowed something so unkosher that my sin is unredeemable. I boiled my own children to serve to a good-for-nothing husband. The Greeks say somebody did that; it might have been me.

New Age tells me I can change the matrix of my disease. Chocolate kisses won't cure me, however; neither will avoidance, like checking out one more whodunit from the library. Placebos result only in postponement. I must confront my illnesses like cookie crumbs in the bed, not roll over them as if they did not exist. I'd better not lower the blinds, as my widowed grandmother did to hide from an unwanted suitor. I could treat my ulcer with hypnosis, relaxation, meditation, biofeedback, imagery, acupuncture, workshops, seminars, and other psychotechnologies. I could join the Gray Panthers and struggle for elder rights. I could exorcise the family cancers with primal screams.

A Venus Flytrap

Bibles—Old or New—and Korans are infallible. Holistic priests and priestesses may be Christian, Jewish, Sufi, or Muslim. Holism swallows up whatever lies in its path, like a woman-eating plant. It's a code word, a badge of belonging to New Age, not Old Age.

I'll convert! Christian preachers float up in the holistic soup while Kabbala mystics sink like matzo balls.

The Humpty Dumpty Syndrome

Seeking after wholeness, my parts are strewn all over the page. It's the Humpty Dumpty syndrome, in a straight line from Adam. Once we had the glossy perfection of the egg—that is, before the Fall. Is fragmentation Old Age or Modern Age? For some, the Modern Age began around 1851; for others, 1900. Then we had Postmodern, its salient point a sense of humor, as in: color a Greek temple with Crayolas, then gut the walls.

There is no humor in the "whole earth" of holism. There are prayers and mantras and spells obscurantist as tea leaves. There is humor in the

Talmud. There is no humor in Jesus. Genius, mercy, and truth, but humor? Show me.

Holists take themselves as seriously as Christians and Muslims. Such religious devotees proselytize for conversion to the one, the only faith. So do holists. They would never accept the newest Magic Markers, engineered to rub off. Religion doesn't take well to changing *its* mind, only *ours*.

Honey's In, Sugar's Out

With trembling limbs, I wait outside the Holist Gate, trying to stifle my sugar craving and hide my unzipped handbag crammed with pills. I should have brought a knapsack or fanny pack. When I see the Angel of Death in blinding light, a crystallization of old Valium, do I say, wait? We'll try a holistic approach: Let the mind catch up with the body; treat the patient, not the disease; the symptom is not the total condition; matter and energy are linked. Just let me collect my pieces.

Living holistically should be easier than dying. I might try a weekend seminar called Windows to the Sky (subtitled Past-Life Regression). Admission's been reduced by three hundred dollars. They swear that I can break the pattern, move off the Karmic wheel, and clear the blocks in consciousness that have "tainted" my outlook. I can make contact with my higher soul self. This is not a job for extra-strength acetaminophen.

My Bypass

I bypassed *The Holistic Health Handbook* for the titlistically more comprehensive *Holistic Health Lifebook: A Guide to Personal and Planetary Well-Being*. As my readers will have deduced, I'm having such trouble with "personal" that I'm not sure I can upgrade to "planetary." I do pray that I can deal with "mind-spirit" without getting into "spiritual," but that doesn't seem realistic. The New Age landscape is irradiated with self-righteousness.

Will I Never Achieve Systemic Harmony?

Caught between grassroots populist medicine and the AMA, where do I go? Even Hippocrates had his ups and downs with dogmatics, skeptics, and empiricists. Am I now ready for ecotopia?

I have a friend financially and spirit-consciously involved with forms of energy. She dug her own well, sells windmills, and promotes consumer ownership and management of electricity. Could I really live without utilities as enemies? I so look forward to opening my gas and electric bills, primed for the rage I require.

Am I any more of a hypocrite than Frank Lloyd Wright, father of the proposed utopian, though horizontal, Broadacres City, who spent years trying to finance the construction of a mile-high skyscraper?

The Paradigm of the Urban Village

I should be a prime candidate for the urban village, where plants feed humans from the nutrients humans have fed them. Why am I not motivated to use water hyacinths for producing recreational water out of sewage? Am I against hyacinths? Do I have a superior plan for waste? I feel irrelevant as the streets that could be converted into organic farm acreage. Think of the subsidies!

From my reading, I have pegged myself as a nonsynergic nerd who, despite feeling economically exploited, does not look to community to find my alpha and omega. I am too involved in personhood as a social goal. Will I ever choose hug tag over Monopoly? In hug tag, the only time you're safe is when you're hugging another player. In Monopoly, the only time I feel safe is when I own Boardwalk *and* the utilities.

Is 4,000 Years Ago Tomorrow?

A brain researcher suggests that in the holographic state—the frequency domain—4,000 years ago could be tomorrow. If it is, then what I see in the mirror is merely a holograph sixty-seven years young. I won't have to establish a relationship with plants or go through paradigm upheaval. I could skip Roswell's celebration of the alleged UFO alien landing of forty years ago, along with dehydration, heat stroke, snakebite, assault weapons, handguns, and T-shirts.

I could bypass Clairvoyant Counsel, transformation, stress reduction, acu-yoga, and Fat Liberation. Without divine grace and the planetarization of consciousness, I could slobber for millennia in sentient being and still not achieve millenarian . . . even if I get home in time for the 6 P.M. news.

Chapter Six

Spiritual Fuel

Confession Digression

On Sunday mornings in a Southwestern town noted for its plethora of art galleries and tensions among Anglos, Indians, and Hispanics, several hundred refugees from 12-step programs assemble in the School for the Deaf auditorium. Their mood is more than hopeful; it is ecstatic.

Hand clapping and foot stomping, they yell out, "I love you," the group mood both revival meeting and rock concert, a New Age postcard of rainbows and reassurance. Their hymns are taken not from God or Buddha or Jesus (who failed to make the cut), but from such '60s icons as Bob Dylan and Peter, Paul, and Mary.

In contrast with the youth attending the love-ins of the '60s, the age range in this gathering extends from whelp to wheelchair. I recognize seniors who once danced bare-breasted on the nude dunes of California, or stormed the halls of Berkeley with banners demanding free speech. Some leftovers can still be seen at the original sites, shivering and wrapped in Navajo blankets, by New Age purveyors of beads and bangles and incense and thirty-year-old tie-dyed T-shirts.

Far from the Last Chance Ranch

Seniors in the School for the Deaf auditorium are distinguished from baby boomers by the dying fire in their eyes. They are roomers at the Last Chance Ranch. They do not leap from stage to audience like the longhaired thirty-something leading a double life as weekday wolf in stockbroker Armani and weekend confession junkie.

Another thirty-something has lost his bird, surrogate for the grown-up love he finds too challenging; the feathered fetish expired on a camping junket. This boomer is comforted in the arms of a peer who recently lost his canine companion. The dual tribute to animal loyalists is greeted by fervid catcalls of support as the two limp off together.

A middle-aged woman, professionally successful in the penal system, revels in a tale of parental sexual abuse. Not to worry—God has appeared in full Technicolor glory. Screamed hallelujahs belie the nondenominational claims of the nonreligious service.

Why I Am Here

I have been invited by a peer whose eyes were aglow with revelation. What do unattached senior singles do on Sunday mornings if they scorn the funnies and TV pundits? If on Saturday our sins are redeemed by car-washing or lubrication, dry-cleaning pickups, and grocery shopping, Sunday is a hole in the heart of misbelievers. Especially those who can't leap from proscenium to audience without breaking both legs as a result of calcium deficiency.

Sunday reaches out not just to fellow seniors but to dropouts of every generation. Sunday is three o'clock all day, when the crucifixion hour looms and Moses' tablets appear broken as bread. A sixty year old—who at six feet in height kicks off her shoes to sing—is radiant with self-transfiguration, she who was silent for nearly six decades. Her professed agony at self-exposure is contradicted by the easy delivery. She is mobbed by well-wishers.

Revelation

Revelation is the keynote of a "poem" read to thunderous applause by a pretty actress with professional stage makeup. Sentimental to a fault, the piece is greeted like a bone from a 9,000-year-old Peruvian girl, or a lost fragment from the Dead Sea Scrolls. My peers appear transfigured like tots by a birthday cake, comatose from the sugar.

All this revelation seems so effortless. If only I had been abused by my father. If only I had lost my little bird. Or my dog. (I have had uneasy relationships with canines ever since I was bitten as a baby in a carriage. Or was that attack just a metaphor for infancy?)

If only I could sing like an angel in a halo while crying that I hurt. Atheism is dead. It's not only dead; it's passé. I have tried affiliating with the nonaffiliated, and I have failed. I remain unconverted.

Celebration does not work in my case. I even lost the one who invited me to the feast. The next day, bitching about arthritis, cat allergies, smoke, foul air, the lack of unattached men on the local scene, and an endless list of foods she cannot tolerate, she breathes into her oxygen mask for fragrance disorder, lifting it off only to complain, "Enough. I won't listen to you. I will only open my ears to *joy*."

She's right. Joy should be contagious like the common cold. So I should not keep my eyes closed. Since celebration is not working, I could try joy hypnotherapy, which includes—in addition to group hypnosis, numerology, and tarot—Eye Movement Densensitization Reprocessing, a procedure harder to say than to practice. Joy hypnotherapy promises to "unite the personality to the universal source of divine consciousness." But on Sunday, a day of rest?

I'll have to solve the Sunday morning dilemma, now that I've turned down ambrosia. Sleep in, maybe, or mix up a fruit smoothie with Citrucel. Or is it time to pass the hemlock?

Thirteen Flights to Oblivion

If Old Agers ask, "What is the answer?" New Agers counter with, "What is the question?" The first hints at a wailing wall; the second strives to reframe the dialogue between soul the laureled athlete and soul the cop-out.

A friend of mine died two years ago. E. was the female pope of the possible. At age seventy-five, she dreamed of a face-lift that would bring suitors scurrying to bed and wed her. Unable to round up the down payment for cosmetic surgery, she devised an alternate plan to postpone a visit from the Reaper. Her plan bore some resemblance to Nancy Reagan's Just Say No tactic to stamp out drugs. This Pythagorean scheme assumes that where there's smoke there will be fire.

E. had published seventeen books, mostly by cajoling and threatening publishers, as well as staging walkouts, boycotts, and indomitable reappearances. A self-taught writer, she did not recognize the word *no*. E. reacted to arthritis by staging marathons on a Stairmaster of her own devising. Gymnastic machines were too flat and confining. Outside her apartment door lay her Himalayan range—cresting on her own, the thirteenth, floor. Each morning, oblivious to weather or pains in the joints, she trotted down thirteen terraced levels and then up again like a mailman.

Now You See Her, Now You Don't

As my guest in San Francisco, waving a two-fer coupon from a giveaway paper, E. invited me to lunch in Chinatown. There would be no taxi; we would take the subway to save money. Besides, the subway was only a block and a half from my house. When we got off at our downtown stop, she disappeared. Growing more and more anxious, I spent fifteen or twenty minutes searching the station. Finally, she trotted up in her sweats—the same outfit she'd worn on her arrival and the only one she'd brought for a three-and-a-half-day stay.

Her expression was beatific. Missing her San Diego Everest, she had, with New Age zest, been running up and down the escalator stairs! Six months later she was dead of lung cancer.

What Has This to Do with Spirituality?

To understand how E's demise relates to contemporary spirit quests, ask the long-distance runner whose endorphins kick in after five miles or ten. Or the racing car driver whose concussions inspire visions unseen by ordinary mortals.

As for my friend, I should mention that for twenty-five years she was a three-pack-a-day smoker, and that she had quit as many years before. The body's memory is relentless as Yeats's savage God.

While E., like most aging New Agers, was sure she could beat the odds, the debt collector waited in the shadow at the bottom of the stairs like an all-too-patient pederast.

A Glimpse of Olympus

So even Olympians fall. But a torch was lit. E. had convinced the Olympic Committee to sponsor three volumes of rhyme by contemporary master poets. On a scant widow's pension, tapping out her demands on an old Royal portable, she bludgeoned into submission a stellar cast of Nobel and Pulitzer writers and an international cast of CEOs for her board of directors. Keeping track of pennies for postage, she took in contributions from all over the world, she who taught at a major California university without (I suspect) a college degree.

This might have been an inspiring tale of the power of Old Age to conquer fate . . . except for the thirteen flights of stairs, which gave to a New Age lady what the decathlon gave to the ancient Greeks—a glimpse of Olympus.

Transplant Transmigration

History bustles with migrations. They are not, as some believe, a twentieth-century phenomenon. Our own continent was peopled with invaders who (allegedly) crossed the Bering land bridge. Recent research, questioning if these were in fact Asians, proposes that they may instead have been blue-eyed Caucasoids from what is now Western Europe. In the

Southwestern United States, where I've migrated to, Native Americans hotly dispute this theory. Their creation myths identify them as the earliest peoples on the North American land mass. There we were trying to close down their casinos and now we are abducting their ancestors. For shame.

In North America immigration proceeds apace. Now the Asians knock again at our portals. Whether we look at Europe, Africa, or Asia, a massive people-wall moves in nearly every direction, victims of flood, famine, or drought, of genocide and shifting borders.

While immigrants from Cambodia or Haiti or Zaire move here to work, reproduce, or die, an aging population blessed with the mobility granted by financial means and reasonable health, migrates to new centers of energy of a different sort. Something is missing. As people live longer, another knot has appeared on the trunk of the Tree of Life—an itch, a dissatisfaction sometimes called *Is this all there is?*

Virtually Spiritual

People move to new energy centers both physically and mentally. The church can be a supermarket, a theater, or an auditorium. It can be a forest or field or mountain where ancient nature spirits are once again propitiated in sunrise ceremonies or moonlit orgies.

When people ask what brought me to Santa Fe, I say without hesitation, "The land." I do not seek to *own* land, I add, but to *look at* it. Yet I spend ninety percent of my moving hours driving up and down a noisy strip of malls, getting and spending, wasting my powers.

This Place Crawls with Women of a Certain Age

The women here look so like me that I do a double take. We cluster on the rim of this town like fruit flies on a sticky jar. There are men here (the women say not nearly enough of them) with the same itch. Those who need less congestion drift north to Taos; those who need to make a living, south to Albuquerque or back to New York or California.

A publisher of New Age books gave up Manhattan corporate salons to write his own interpretation of what's new, but still hasn't a clue.

Instead, he prints the wisdom of peyote eaters who lead the way in the spiritual dimension. He has dropped the Armani suit for Gabby Hayes boots, jeans, and an unfocused expression. Men like him are accompanied by longhaired nymphs one third their age. Men like him (and women too) are engaged in virtual spirituality. They collect Santa Clara pottery, or Plaza paintings. They wear turquoise-studded watches and belts with enough semiprecious stones to buy Manhattan Island.

Spiritual Must Mean Religious

Here, where Christ and his *santos* infest hand-carved *retablos,* they are art, not life. The shakier the drawing or modeling, the more its price rises . . . a sort of virtual art. Museums and collectors vie for the showiest pieces. By the time the Spanish Fair opens to the public, the best ones are taken. Children are paid several hundred dollars for the crudest crafts.

All this makes for a fitting revenge on the swarming Anglos who have raised the price of rice and tacos. A revenge in hacked wood, smeared paint, and rings that may lose their semiprecious stones in one wearing.

Tourists frequent the churches, ministered to by local guides. Churches are not "spiritual" to the less newly arrived; long pleated broom skirts are, crushed velvet in midsummer. Closetfuls of boots, conch belts (leather with silver "shells"), bolo ties, and sombreros. Roadrunners and thunder patterns. Ethnic clothing, Afghanistan rugs, "wearable" art—all surface with little style or structure. Decorated gourd auctions. Concerts on public basketball courts where the jovial conductor harangues us that his unpaid musicians cannot finish the Haydn until larger donations march up to the "stage."

The Youth-Deprived

Virtual spirituality is a godsend to the youth-deprived. A heart and lung transplant. A ladder of ascension to the higher realms—hence the angel greeting cards, wrapping paper, and hit TV programs. Angels have survived the auto-da-fé of organized religions. Angels must be virtual as well as virtuous. Heaven is as virtual as it gets.

Chapter Seven

The Ethereal—
or Material?—Girl

Pop the Madonna

Before maternity, Madonna was the Material Girl. New Age, we'll agree. Bras worn outside shirts. No, not bras, but bustieres. That was before maternity set in.

We JAPs (Jewish American Princesses) were material girls before Madonna was born. Cadillacs by the half dozen. Hairdresser on Saturday morning. Sex on Saturday night. The only ethereality we knew was as beautiful brides. We saved the hymeneal pair from the cake. Sugar was forever. After that, it was Monday stenography and Friday pay days. Someone destroyed the heavenly city and bombed Eden along with Dresden. Consumption wasn't so bad; ask today's fasters. Hunger is pervasive, which doesn't mean it's authentic.

If bones can regrow in seven years, then broken hearts should mend. Ask the cardiologist. I'm not sure whether anyone has photographed the passage of a soul, in arrival *or* departure.

In saving the environment, I'm told by some, we save ourselves.

Suppose I'm a rancher, or a land speculator, or an ordinary grassroots toxic dumper. I'd then say that saving the planet costs too much money. Having spent trillions in land waste and desecration, I'd scare the public with the millions that toxic cleanup and conservation might cost.

I Should Give up Clutter

I should volunteer to live more simply, vow not to bring in shells from the beach. But then, I'm kept up all night with regret for all those I left— even after the ones I've occasionally brought home have dried out and dulled. Maybe volunteer simplicity is not my *shtick*. My house is over- crowded. The more I lose, the more I keep. I'm a conspicuous consumer, after any cork in a storm. And I can't even drink. My low tolerance for alcohol ebbed out in the '80s. Or it might have been the '70s when, after mixing tequila sunrises, I spent the night throwing my boyfriend's furni- ture over the balcony. In the '90s, I forget the ends of words, but never the notice of a sale.

Ethereal . . . me? I don't think so. I'm sick to death of angels, who are everywhere except where they belong. And now we're asked to give up sugar—a plot by Lucifer, for sure, with CIA connivance, to dynamite the Cuban market. The government's still fixated on Castro.

I read that voluntary simplicity depends on an attitude, not a budget. The New Age is romantic, turning frogs into princes. Lace and sequins on denim—etherealization requires lots of lace. In the transformative process, content should lead to relevance, fragmentation to integration.

Learning is a process, not a product. The product is JOY—a state that cannot be expressed in lower case letters. JOY is sublimity, dream jour- nals, storytelling, a magic mushroom or peyote ground.

Forget the fear of flying. The spaceship is already airborne. The new paradigm informs a fresh curriculum. Let your hair frizz. Prepare for the transition into planetary culture. Transform for transcendence, for the cherubim and seraphim of Levi, transcriber of the Akashic Records. Communicate with spirit planes. Find your spirit guides beckoning from over the cloud rim. They may not be human; they could be tigers, coyotes, crows, panthers, or hanged men from tarot cards. You don't have to be influenced by Freud or Jung or English Freemasons or Egyptian theurgy or the Order of the Golden Dawn. You're just asked to believe before you're handed material proof.

Seventeenth-Century Chamber Pots

See how easily the material obliterates the ecstatic. You'll be told that you need to read *Conversations with God* to improve your relationship with God, friend and lover. Tap the human potential movement. Natural over unnatural. A seance table. A hip masseuse. If peyote is out, try celery root, antimony for cleansing. According to Aldous Huxley, seventeenth-century chamber pots were searched for precious purgatives to be reused from generation to generation. Huxley reminded us of Paracelsus, the anti-Galenist physician who claimed that just "as antimony purifies gold and leaves no slag in it, in the same form and shape it purifies the human body."[1]

Ethereal spheres postulate other delights for the universal mind. Visualize astral havens. Indulge in auras. Thoreau and Whitman went transcendental, as did our Founding Fathers, members of a secret society that dabbled in Rosicrucian fusion.

Orgasm May Be the End All

Men promise orgasmic delights to seduce us. A little poke or tickle will cure headaches, cramps, and mortgage problems. According to psychologist Wilhelm Reich, orgasms are the path to rejuvenation and renewal. Bhagwan Shree Rajneesh marketed the orgasmic vision in dancing meditations and free play. Release is equated with self-healing—as is its opposite, suppression, claimed by Tantric practitioners and early Christian Gnostics to increase sexual pressure. Both methods ensure the attainment of cosmic heights.

The celibacy of the Gnostics aimed to channel orgone/Kundalini energy into spiritual organs. Yet ecstatic states are also associated with shamanic trance. Catalysts for these altered states of consciousness are hypnosis and endorphins.

Shamans and Neoplatonists

Hypnosis achieved via biofeedback techniques can induce certain forms of meditation. Endorphins regulate pain and temperature, influence perceptions of pleasure and mood, regulate drives, and may influence memory of an event. Acupuncture triggers the release of endorphins, as do stress, vigorous motor activity, suggestion, or prolonged sensory stimulation.

Should we become jaded with the shaman's altered state of consciousness, we could always go back to Neoplatonism's spiritual plane of the Ideal. Shamans are triggered by communication with animal alter egos met while climbing cloud ladders. The difference between the shaman's journey and the psychotic's lies in the exercise of control. Shaman Michael Harner describes a brush with the sublime in *The Way of the Shaman: A Guide to Power and Healing*.

Perhaps holistic healing is a form of shamanic quest; but then, so is insanity. In the acting out of psychodrama, there may be some grunting and thrashing. Healing can be picturesque as well as Pinteresque. The line between drama and melodrama is drawn by the actor.

Part Two

Feeding
the Mammal

Chapter Eight

Nourishing the Self-Righteous

You Are What You Eat

In the late '60s my son first uttered the catechism You are what you eat—a mantra for wholeness, breathtaking in its *chutzpah*. For here was the nut popped from the shell, the primal link between mind, soul, and intestines for which humans had been searching, reduced to a catch phrase, an instant formula that connected digestion and elimination with religion like $e=mc^2$.

Soon afterward, I was greeted with mirror images reflecting choice: *What I eat becomes me; therefore, I become what I eat.* No more mommy screaming in us that we must eat our spinach or liver. We're in control now. That's what New Age is about, where it's moved on to from the primal scream.

Now *I* choose the menu and do the cooking. After six decades, I've reached the advanced stage of a two-and-a-half year old who decides what she will and won't eat. Mommy, stand back while I throw your foods from the high chair, or smear them on your face.

The Organic Emporium

Organic has gone from shed to mainstream, from a hole in the wall in Boulder or Berkeley to brightly lit boutiques in Bakersfield and Fresno, playing one-upsmanship with supermarkets that ape its products and marketing.

In Giant markets, signs of this copycat mentality can be found in platoons of wood-and-plastic bins packed with whole grains, brown rice, dried fruits, nuts, and that unmistakable emblem of New Age, trail mix. For hikers about to trek the 1,000-mile Appalachian Trail or the cannibalistic Donner Pass, or looking for survival snacks to get them through the urban clot, trail mix has been the answer.

What *Is* in Trail Mix

In addition to a variety of nuts and seeds, trail mix is known for its raisins. No ordinary raisins, those in trail mix are upscale, sanctified originally by purveyors of foodstuffs who were not professional grocers. These New Agers drove pickup trucks. They picketed against nuclear fuel while they picked at guitars, not violins. They formed food co-ops, and leafleted against nonorganic, teeming as it was with pesticides and pollution. They used the term "macrobiotic" like a chemical weapon. They worshipped food so much that they fasted to avoid masticating it; like Saint Catherine, they boasted that eating pus was wholesome.

How to Be Sure It's Organic

There are five ways to know for sure that food is organic:
1. The sign says so.
2. Organic costs two to three times as much as nonorganic.
3. Organic has imperfections. (None of those glossy tomatoes sprayed with preservatives like blow-up sex dolls.) Look for rot and decomposition.
4. Look for the aura. Organic fruits fester with self-satisfaction.
5. When in doubt, ask. *Warning*: You'll perceive a look of pity from the clerk, implying that you're an innerterrestrial nerd.

Caution: Eating May Be Unnatural

What, then, is natural? Ask General Foods, which has usurped the word to cover even chemical additives. If you're a natural woman or man, you'd better eat your daily oat bran.

Natural is the password to New Age paradise. *Paradise* is from the Persian Zoroastrian *pairi daeza*, meaning enclosure. The right food has its own halo, marking the sacred precinct of harps.

On the back of a bottle of iced tea are a series of catechisms: "100% Natural" and, in larger, more contrasting letters below it, "Real Brewed." The word *real* has intimations of virtual reality (see chapter 14). Back to natural . . . On either side of the flavor's name (peach) are twin claims: "Naturally Flavored" (appealing to the left brain) and "With Other Natural Flavors" (appealing to the right brain). "Other" is troublesome as an undocumented alien. But let's pass on to "Contains No Juice—All Natural." Is juice unnatural?

Farther down we find "Natural Flavors and Fruit Pectin." By now, we have encountered *natural* five times. Who would dare call the bottle's contents unnatural, especially since there is a sixth *natural* to be found on the front label: "All-Natural Iced Tea," followed by the vow that it was "brewed with pure water and the finest ingredients."

This iced tea sounds like a worthy candidate for Eden, notwithstanding its "Nutrition Facts." These include calories (110), total fat (0 g, 0%, exactly what the nutrition cops yearn to hear), sodium (5 mg, 0%, another winner!), total carb (26 g, 9%), sugars (26 g!), and protein (0 g, so why mention it?).

More Nutrition Zaps

Let's move on to a cereal box. I've given up even before checking the side panel, for who can quarrel with the holy cow "Nutrition"? The word is unassailable. We're back to eating what mommy said was good for us. As for "wheat," we're not told whether it's bleached or unbleached. I don't dare ask how much wheat; it could be .000000000001%. But then, we cannot quarrel with a "Fact."

I scanned a pancake mix box to see if it contained eggs. After reading off twenty-six ingredients, I stopped from sheer exhaustion, just before the culprit "eggs." My strictly vegetarian son shuddered when his more exhaustive search beheld the twenty-seventh ingredient, to which he's philosophically allergic. Next time I'll sneak off to I Hop for pancakes while he tears into his organic grapefruit.

The "Others"

I first discovered the "others" while reading a fabric label required by law to divulge fiber content. After cotton, linen, and rayon, I found the mysterious "other (2%)." This could be the component that bursts into flame or that when wet smells like rotten eggs.

"Others" are our mystery guests. How does calcium phosphate differ from monocalcium phosphate, or from sodium aluminum phosphate, or dicalcium phosphate? Are there good and bad phosphates? And what are phosphates doing in my pancake mix? There's aluminum too—which I thought belonged in the pot, not its contents. I have to take a chemistry course before I can eat my breakfast.

In *50⁺: The People's Pharmacy for Older Adults* I am warned that phosphates can make me more susceptible to broken bones. As for aluminum, it grabs on to phosphate internally and may even deplete it. And all this is perfectly "natural."

At least Kellogg's has got the sweetener covered. *Wheat and honey* is politically correct. (Can you imagine selling a wheat-and-*sugar* pancake mix?) One thing more: there's a pat of butter simmering on the stack on the front of the box. I'd feel more confident in its New Age credentials if I knew it was goat butter. Or yak butter. Cows can decorate dish towels, but in the skillet they're politically incorrect.

Vitamins and Supplements

Vitamins are a fairly new discovery. But they're not simple. Authors Joe and Teresa Graedon, among others, point out how persnickety vitamins can be. With vitamin E comes the sinister warning, "Have your doctor check your bleeding time." Vitamin K depletion leads to bleeding gums; yet we are warned not to binge on foods rich in vitamin K, because they block the action of blood thinners. We are advised not to gulp down megadoses of selenium, copper, or vitamin B-6 or D. Beta-carotene pills or carrots? One testimonial came from a devotee who forced beta-carotene and vitamins to offset the "mutagenic effects" of food.

A word about aging and vitamin D: if you're a senior, stay out in the sun, since it converts raw nutrients into vitamin D, increasing your calcium uptake. But don't stay out too long or you'll increase your chances of skin cancer. If you hate the sun or live close to the North Pole, eat lots of sardines.

If You Hate Sardines

If you are afraid of smelling fishy, try herbs—they're deep *ch'i* builders. *Ch'i* is the Chinese word for life force, but you don't have to be Chinese to enjoy shitake mushrooms any more than you have to be Jewish to like Levy's rye bread. Still, mushrooms alone may not cut it. For deeper *ch'i* and increased immunity, it may be advisable to add maitake to your shi-take, along with reishi, ginger, and Siberian ginseng. If the mix appears too pan-Asian, or if you lack immigration documents, try a sprinkling of California spikenard.

Is Wheat Germ a Form of Chemical or Biological Warfare?

While we're on the subject of foreign issues, we had better confront wheat germ. Although "wheat" may be a coverup; it's the "germ" that troubles me. The word may refer to "a disease-causing microorganism" or "a portion of an organism capable of developing into a new one." Wheat germ, whether biological or chemical, is a form of New Age warfare, an attempt to stick New Age *shtick* into a population of nonbelievers like me.

Wheat Germ Isn't the Only Culprit

There's a guy who stuffs himself with megavitamins and beta-carotene because he says food causes cancer. Eating is like shooting bullets into your DNA, he notes, its effects like those of atomic radiation. This isn't science fiction—you're a factory of exponentially reproducing radioactivity. Each time you stuff your mouth, it's like strapping on a pack of terrorist bombs. This guy infers that eating is self-immolation. In other words, food kills!

The Fountain of Youth

Can we outrun the genetic clock? Can we repair DNA like we can the family car? Can vitamin supplements or other substances like SOD (superoxide dismutase, a naturally produced free-radical scavenger) extend our lives? Free radicals are implicated in diabetes, cancer, rheumatoid arthritis, and coronary artery disease. But increased intakes of antioxidants and free-radical–scavenging enzymes have not extended the life of lab animals, though they do multiply profits for manufacturers.

Forgetfulness is a harbinger of death. If brain cells begin dying at birth, they don't have to be so obvious about it later on. Memory pills that speed up the flow of oxygen to the brain are in the offing to reverse or slow down dementia.

Macrobiotics and Youth

Maybe we should stop looking for the Fountain of Youth and instead wok-cook a mound of brown rice. When the diet is macro, its users are micro-thin. The skeletal torso of Gandhi on an ultimate fast was my first glimpse at the macro diet effect. Dr. Roy Walford, author of *The 120-Year Diet*, suggests undernutrition as a way to postpone death. It appears that mice live longer when they eat less . . . but then, they don't live very long to begin with.

Chapter Nine

Diet . . . or Die

Holistic Diet

With the plethora of material published on nutrition and its corollary, living longer, laypeople could be easily confused. We've already seen that to join the Aquarians, we must think, and eat, holistically. To me, as a pragmatic feet-on-the-ground, head-in-the-clouds person, nutrition can be explained in terms of two principles: what goes in must come out and what goes up must come down.

What Goes in Must Come out

What is eaten or drunk must be expelled. Ever since Adam's Fall, we've become human cesspools tainted with disease. Remember Edgar Cayce's recipe for the cure: a high colonic (enema) to rid us of the sins that manifest in disease.

That isn't all, for there are other forms in which the ingested emerges. For instance, there is fat. Once, fat was revered, as in "the fat of the land." Such plenty is now despised. Less is more. If you don't believe this, look at the millions earned by models Christie Brinkley and Naomi Campbell. The Cs in their names do not stand for cellulite, that spongelike jellyfish arising subcutaneously in bumps and lumps to parody our swimsuit delusions.

Five Steps for Deconstructing Cellulite

Successful attacks on embarrassing cellulite follow a series of five steps. First, denial ("It can't be"). Second, anger and frustration ("Why me?"). Third, depression ("It isn't fair"). Fourth, bargaining ("If you'll just stay underground tonight, we'll both forget it ever happened"). Finally, there comes acceptance. Don't kid yourself into thinking this last step is passive. Acceptance of the solution doesn't imply an acceptance of the problem.

Solutions to Wrinkles, Bags, and Fat

Which approach to wrinkles, bags, and fat appears to be most radical—cut & stitch (a wearable art solution), heave and be kneaded, or diet or die (New Age or Old Age)? Let's consider them one by one.

Cut & Stitch

There's no avoiding the question that arises when women (and male TV anchormen) of a certain age congregate: Is face-lift New Age? Although Edgar and Shirley assert that we are perfect, our mirrors tell a different story, the tale of gravity's pull—not a Norman Mailer title, but a fact of science. What goes up must come down like the Roman Empire. Gravity is no respecter of gender. This boob was at chest level yesterday. Where did it go?

That is where science comes in, at least for those with discretionary income. If the machine is too slow, the knife must scrape and slice. Easy and quick as cutting a rug.

Will the knife take enough? And how much is enough? Are you left with a mask too taut to drink or speak? If so, try follow-up surgery! A friend just out of her post-op football helmet was rhapsodizing about the next cut. Megadose vitamins for surgery prep had left her militant, a career soldier ready for the next onslaught. Although she and the surgeon had agreed to stop short of tight-as-a-drum, he didn't remove enough skin, she said.

If he had, I wondered, would she still be able to smile or brush her teeth? Twenty thousand dollars used to buy us a house, then a car. On a face (despite the smaller square footage) it's now a down payment.

How much is enough? is the wrong question. Here's the right one: _Is too much enough?_ Surgery, like exercise, is addictive. Foreplay replaces orgasm. Means become ends. The knife as savior? New Age would shudder, preferring deep tissue massage or beating the face to remind it to behave.

While falling-in faces evoke confrontation, lumpy thighs call forth visions of a giant liposuction pump, the Old Age bloodhound more intent on fat than gore. Fat is fury embedded in lard. Dieting might help, and again it might not. Besides, it takes too long. Most of us are like my friend in Easthampton who doesn't have forty years to reproduce Giverny from seed. He wants instant Monet.

Plastic versus Cosmetic Surgery is not a New Age solution to Old Age wrinkles and bags. Yet the face does not seem to tolerate the super vacuum cleaner applied to stomach and thigh. Should my friend have had her chakras opened instead? How many chants would have made a difference after a half century of dietary abandon? Is fat an illness . . . or Cayce's "sin"?

New Age or not, wrinkles and bags can be moderated by cosmetic surgery. The word _cosmetic_ is instructive. Forget the drugstore counter with its powders, rouges, and lotions. That sort of camouflage went out with Old Age. New Age requires that for a natural look, paint is not the answer. If you paint the walls of a collapsing house, you're wasting your money. Gut the house! Or at least, remodel. We don't mean just a tuck here and there. That was the old plastic surgery. Compare _plastic_ with _cosmetic,_ its younger upscale sister. Plastic implied that you could correct an injury. The results didn't have to be gorgeous. Plastic was Third Avenue; cosmetic is Park Avenue, Upper East Side. But both are Old Age.

Psychic Surgery Is New Age We've been asking the wrong questions. There's a third and only New Age choice: psychic surgery. This procedure requires neither knife nor surgeon, but rather a transmedium. Rest assured that no blood or tissue will be removed. What, then, are you paying for? For removal of the "spiritual and etheric bodies." The transmedium will be accompanied by both a licensed acupuncturist and a Doctor of Oriental Medicine. From a trans-Asian perspective, it's kosher. The trauma is to your checkbook. The beginning seminar alone might set you back three-fifty.

Heave and Be Kneaded

Enter the machine age, complete with rowing machine, stair-climbing machine, sit-up machine and lie-down machine, ski machine, treadmill, and promise-keeper universal. The latter is a unified field theory term willed by Einstein to New Age—which brings us back to wholeness, and ab fulfillment.

The Old Age reducing salon has been replaced by a new church: the gym. You won't recognize it, for it resembles a fern bar. If you're thirsty, try a seaweed smoothie. While you sip, enjoy the groaning and moaning, the porno song of the saved—saved from drooping boobs and buns, cheating husbands, and the cellulite craze. Exercise is a seven-day-a-week obsession. It swallows up your spare time along with excess pounds. You can even buy your own treadmill on a lifetime installment plan. You can climb K-2 while watching Jane Fonda's video. It's like being reborn. Or having sex at home, alone.

Exercise Is the New Messiah

Exercise brings hope, but it works best alongside diet. Like Buddha with Jesus, or Lao-tzu beside a yogi. More satisfying than a third husband, exercise is where It is, thumbing its nose at Old Age. Drag on the shiny tights; they hide unexplained knobs and varicose veins. In the gym you can win.

Outdoors, the whole world is your track. You can power walk or power run, and drive drivers crazy. Take your weights and jog. All you need is your sleek neon outfit, a Walkman, a bottle of water, and the right shoes. Michael Jordan has hundreds, but you need only two. Just follow your very own guru, huffing, puffing, chugging to Nirvana. Stop and take your pulse. You've done it, outstrode Father Time, mixing the old and new like silicone on a natural base—a merger of Martha Stewart with Rod.

The Medium Is the Massage . . . and Sometimes the Masseuse

The laying on of hands is sacred to New Agers. They seem to require no permission or prior knowledge of the subject. Complain about anything going wrong and they will grab the adjacent portion of your anatomy and begin squeezing, kneading, or otherwise disturbing the body's comfortably out-of-kilter kinks to make an "adjustment." Call them Sunday chiropractors, although they will stalk you day and night spouting New Age adages.

"Hmm . . . feels tight here." *Crack* goes the adjustment. Are they licensed? Who knows? They are our neighbors, lovers, clerks, clients, strangers. *Crack. Crack.* "How does that feel?" It hurts! I could cut off their hands at the wrists. Who asked them to disrupt my normal neuroses?

Diet or Die

When it comes to this solution, my favorite book title is *Lifespan-Plus: 900 Natural Techniques for Living Longer.* As if 900 techniques were not enough, we are advised of 101 foods to help extend our lives. Why not 100? New Age oversells.

The book's flyleaf accuses us of cutting short our 120-year life-span potential by nearly half. It exhorts us to rejuvenate our hearts, stay infection-free, prevent a stroke, strengthen our bones, eliminate body toxins! Among its chapter headings are "Live Lean," "Live Longer," and "Life without Stress." Life extension may be aided by hydralazine (an antitension drug), beta-blockers (heart drugs), and extra-strength laxatives (there's colonic Cayce again).

Walking with weights is ill-advised, as they increase blood pressure. But don't recline or you'll decline. As for reducing stress, my favorite tip is, "Pet your pet." Petting a human sends blood pressure soaring.

Under the image of a billboard bearing the words "Women are the Fatter Sex," the writers caution us to dodge our diet demons. Tips for calorie dodging include not buying food when you're hungry and refusing to meet friends at a restaurant. Don't eat it—freeze it. When the freezer's full, sell it. What counts is not just looking good, but also sticking around to enjoy the effect.

Homeopathic and Other Solutions to Eating A homeopathic antidote to eating could be more eating. Forget grassroots herbalism, kelp
salads, and wholegrain bread. Homeopathy calls for minute doses of
substances that produce the problematic symptoms.

Here's an alternate remedy: eat crumbs instead of lumps, and chew
each crumb twenty-five times. A former employer of mine took up this
practice on the advice of a specialist. Did he lose weight? No, but his jaw
became too sore to chew, so he had to switch to a liquid diet.

A former student took off 125 pounds in a year and a half by giving
up solids. That's another form of past-life regression. Forget the spoon;
try the bottle. Is this holistic? Who cares, as long as it works.

To maintain your holistic purity, try nonfattening foods such as lean
fish, spinach, sprouts, pumpkin, pomegranates, raspberries, nonfat
yogurt—and beware of coworkers bearing donuts. If you're still hungry, try
snowshoeing, or sex. (*Note:* sex is *not* nonfattening if, in disdaining to smoke
the coveted after-sex cigarette, you hit the refrigerator like an invading Gaul.)

Herbology

Herbology is not about a man named Herb. It is about seed-producing
plants that are valued for their medicinal properties. I've always preferred
the sound of *herbaceous*. From there, it's not too far to *vivacious*—the
sprightly, lively quality of green growing things.

After moving to California in the late '70s, it took me some time to
get used to seeing flowers in salad mix, even though while living in
Mexico briefly in the '80s I savored flower soup. Flowers are everywhere
in Mexico, so of course some must fall in the soup. But nasturtium? The
first time I heard of eating flowers it was dandelion, and you know wilt-
ed dandelion stems turn into brown worms. Recently, I was informed
that dandelion has been used to treat multiple sclerosis; that buttercup
juice counters strep, staph, and tuberculosis; and that lady's slipper low-
ers blood pressure. Many plants contain natural antibiotics. One chart
lists 160 herbs for use in common ailments. A text on Chinese herbs lists
250, some of which are toxic.

Plants used for healing are not always ingested. They may be inhaled (aromatherapy) or ground in oils for herbal baths (hydrotherapy). Welsh wildflowers make up Bach's thirty-eight flower remedies, which *are* used internally, often by dropper. These are taken to avert such negative states of mind as fear, indifference, indecision, pride, and aloofness. The holistic idea is that negative mind-sets cause disease.

Admittedly (although not in practice), when it comes to food combining, I tend to think like a kosher Jew. It runs in the family. My son doesn't eat dairy with meat. Nor does he combine fruit with vegetables at one setting, which led me to dub him the kosher vegetarian. So, suggested holistic food combinations remind me that there could be reasons fruit should be eaten separately, but I have forgotten what they are. Herbs appear too pure to combine, though they do and have done so for centuries in food, in tea, and in healing, much as threads do in weaving.

Before Herbology

During my childhood, the generational equivalent of "herb for healing" was spinach, which guaranteed strength to Superman, who after a serving of the mashed leaves was able to leap tall buildings in a single bound. Parsley appeared on everything from turkey breasts to potato salad. Parsley wasn't an herb but a "garnish." Celery leaves were whisked in and out of soup like brooms. Other than that, seasoning came from salt and pepper, or paprika for color. For baking there was cinnamon, clove, and nutmeg. Although tea was prescribed for colds, I never saw naked tea leaves, for they were tucked primly into baggy condoms years before they clogged garbage disposals. For graduations and proms our moms or dates took us to Chinatown to eat eggrolls, not to visit herbalists. Confronted with herbs, Mother would have sniffed suspiciously and pronounced them *goyish*.

Drifting Into Old Age or Dragged There Kicking

I am charmed by New Age's facility with the *materia medica* of healing plants, including their leaves, roots, bark, and flowers. Such was the menu of dispensers of folk medicine as well as innovative practitioners. Samuel Hahnemann tested vegetable, animal, and mineral substances on himself and his family. His 99 substances have grown in our time to 1,000, many of them offered up by the plant kingdom for our personal purification. Note that plants must be picked in a timely manner; poke used in spring salad becomes toxic by summer.

Chinese herbologists divide plants into "hot" and "cold." Cayenne, a hot herb, would be used to bring down winter fever. This sounds no less pungent or colorful than the mustard plasters our mothers used for chest congestion, or the cold rubbing-alcohol that sent our fevers into shock and eventually teeth-chattering chills. Is Old Age a pain that cannot be sedated or the last New Age stage for healing?

Chapter Ten

Fasting

The Ultimate Diet

Why Fast?

The most obvious reason for fasting is to lose weight. Delight in self-denial is one potential reward. You have a choice between short and long fasts, the shortest being twenty-four hours and the longest of uncertain duration. In either case, although you may begin fasting as a form of self-deprivation, in the end there are multiple rewards.

For those obsessed with weight loss, the dropping of pounds is not to be taken lightly. Of course, you'll put those pounds back on again as soon as you pass through the postdiet phase, while your body is adjusting chemically and hormonally to your quixotic will. Before you know it, you may long to be back in your hippo skin.

Advice to Hippos

Remind yourself that weight loss is just one motive for fasting. The literature asserts that you'll feel healthier if you fast with regularity. Then, too, it's not New Age to be fat. Don't argue that chubby-clothing shops have never been more numerous. What you want is not the womanly shape; it's the anorexic pubescent girl's. Health was the reason a nonagenarian gave long ago for fasting one day a week. Throughout that one day he lay abed to give his body and social security check a rest.

Combining diet with exercise can be problematic. Not so with the European spa method, says Dr. Paavo Airola, who claims that his patients can walk five to ten miles daily as long as they follow his juice diet and submit to enemas at least once every twenty-four hours. I'd walk ten miles, too, to get away from that sobering probe.

The Enigmatic Enema

I remember the enema as a terrorist tactic in the hands of my overfed mother, convincing me that colon cleansing is more effective than brainwashing. Nevertheless, some New Agers recommend up to three enemas a day. The presumed health benefits of this approach are twofold: first, to cleanse each nook and cranny in the food tunnel of the filth accumulated since birth; second, to provide an exit path for the toxins that build up during a fast, when rectal excavation becomes difficult.

One writer describes the body's filth as rubbish to be burnt. Another visualizes it in the context of a North Carolina pig farm where each little piggy is in its cell with hardly room to breathe—each piggy a detested morsel, the outcome of overeating. Eliminating toxic waste from the system is assumed by some to ensure effective and permanent weight loss. Eating lots of fruit on an empty stomach is supposed to flush impacted fecal matter from the system. Together, the twin militias of fast and enema are guaranteed by New Age adepts to cure any disease. But if you can't go it alone, resort to starving.

Rejuvenation in Starving

One repeat-fast master describes the high from fasting as equivalent to that of recreational drugs, which he still allows himself at times. This Wall Street vulture envisions himself a primitive hunter who might not find game for days. He and his cohorts promise that after three or four days on water, sauerkraut juice, and fresh vegetable broth—which both exhausts the body's reserves of carbohydrates, or glycogen, and triggers the liver's release of ketones—you, like any true cannibal deprived of flesh, will begin to eat your own fat. Isn't that appetizing?

Picture the ketone elves mobilizing: Acetone, Acetoacetic Acid, and Beta-Hydroxybutyric Acid stoking the fuel from your reserves as they chant, "Burn, baby, burn." Forget the sweats, the bad taste in your mouth, and the nausea. Your skin is breaking out? No problem. Enjoy the thrill of detoxifying!

Of course, if you want to cheat (who doesn't?), you might lose weight through a combination of acupressure, acupuncture, herbs, and Qi Gong, a form of Chinese meditation. This combo is also advertised to combat disorders associated with fat, including high cholesterol, hypertension, coronary heart disease, hormone imbalance, diabetes, depression, fatigue, and menopause (mentioned in some medical texts as a "disorder" and in others as a "disease").

A Conversion Experience

Fasting has achieved cult status. Like nearly all New Age obsessions, it is as Old Age as history. If you're in a fasting cult, you—like the ancient saints, rabbis, Imams, and pagans—can seek sanctification along with rejuvenation. As St. Clement said, "Fasting is better than prayer."

Through purification, your soul will be emptied of matter. You'll have knockout visions. With new spiritual awareness you, like Moses or Daniel or Greek philosophers or the prophets of Islam, will be able to ascend to the gods. Remember the modern dictum Less is more. If body is the temple, soul is the altar before which you crawl. Deny and thrive!

Food for the Soul

Holism maintains a belief in the immortal soul. Although it has not as yet been photographed, don't give up hope. Suggested viewing sites are bedsides in homes and hospitals where someone shows signs of expiring. Listen for hoot owls and unexplained scratching. It is recommended that you avoid feeding a soul embarked on an out-of-body journey, as it will travel better on an empty stomach.

Transmigrating is a lot like swimming or jogging. While preparing for your own adventure, starve but don't eliminate soul food. Give up barbecued ribs and chitterlings; grease doesn't travel well. Prayers have the best mileage records. And chants. Don't be stingy. Throw plenty of *ohms* in the bone bowl; they'll pay off in multiple incarnations. And have patience—neither Rome nor reincarnation was built in a day. Starving is supernatural. Why dig your grave with a knife and fork?

Diet and Death
(More Food for the Soul)

You won't die if you diet, even though such an outcome is implied in *A Message to Sufferers and Sinners.* True, a few have expired on the peaks of withdrawal. But not Ms. Obese, who dieted 249 days in Glasgow. She needed no bagpipes.

Death from holistic diets is rare. Maybe a heart attack here and there. A kidney failure. Lactic acidosis or volvulus of the small bowel. More common is diet angst—its symptom, acute stomach pangs. Antidote: try drawing a death-rebirth model with seven archetypes. Ignore the Wise Old Man, the Great Mother and Father, Heracles, the Ugly Sickness, Satan, and Athene. You're seeking the original organic Garden. Breathe in deeply . . . and exhale. Chew sugarless gum.

Fasting Is Everlasting

You need to purge. As bulemics can testify, fasting goes hand in hand with this urge. To vomit is to exile not only present life experiences but past-life ones as well. Repeat to yourself 100 times, "The urge to purge is therapeutic, not thanatological."

Fasting can be fun. It can make you whole. It will also purify you. But to establish a dynamic balance, you need dietary cleansing. Alfalfa or clover tea is highly recommended. One source says to rock and hum while squatting.

At the top of the inner circle way inside the triangle depicted in a popular New Age diagram is the Divine Child. Bending as directed, you'll either find this child or fall on your face trying.

Fasting Can Lead to Self-Understanding

While fasting, you'll discover things about your inner self you may never have wanted to know. Such as:

1. You're a food factory.
2. You're a garbage disposal.
3. You're a glutton for punishment.
4. Your colon will never forgive you.
5. Those who hated you as a fatty will hate you even more as a Christie Brinkley with halitosis.
6. You'll miss the ketones when they're gone.

Chapter Eleven

Rolf or Golf . . . and Other Bodywork Options

The Sweat Factor

New Age is about options. So is Old Age. One advantage of rolf-ing and other contemporary forms of bodywork is that you don't have to *shlep* around on endless vistas of grass and sweat. JAPs, after all, were taught not to sweat. It was not ladylike. Furthermore, it kept you from securing a husband. Which meant that you had to shave your underarms bare as the skull of an inmate on death row.

There was a time when I could sit in a sauna until I turned beet red and broke out in welts while my overtrained pores held the line and refused to sweat. I had taught them to be sweatless.

Hair Is New Age

Liberation took on new meaning for me when I sat on a beach with my daughter and her roommates as they compared the length of their underarm hair. How could a man love them? They looked like apes. Not so, a room-mate said. Her boyfriend's favorite foreplay was with her armpit forests.

In the mined field of female liberation, was there an inverse relationship between bralessness and hair? Even a famed musical explored hair! Here I was going braless and corsetless, enjoying newfound superiority over those of my gender still encased in the tools of male domination. But hair?

Deep Tissue Massage Monogamy

I should teach myself to go rolfing. My only knowledge of this sport came from a friend in the '70s whose eyes rolled back in an orgasmic trance when the word was mentioned. It came with the term "deep tissue massage" and questions about monogamy. Rolfing took stamina and pain tolerance. "How," I asked, "can you enjoy someone beating you up?" S. looked aloof. I had missed the point.

One rolfing session, I was told, would be worth more than all the years of therapy I'd had. Fifteen years to cure my headaches? At that time I enjoyed telling folks that what really cured my headaches was divorce.

Massage Masochistic

What I came away with was that S. was masochistic. How could you get in touch with your pain by inflicting more pain on yourself? S. replied that what she sought was to get in touch with her inner consciousness. Through letting herself be smacked unconscious? Our relationship was not to survive this test of faith.

But rolfing did, and went on to become one of the dozens of bodywork techniques responsible for exponentially multiplying the number of massage tables in use. Your hamstrings constricted, your pelvis tilted, your feet toe out. Lovers have wearied of your perpetual smile? Your depression's due to postural deformation, not cash flow. Get the energy flowing—the cash is sure to tag along.

Alternatives to Rolfing

If rolfing busts you, or if your muscles are contracting improperly, or if you have diarrhea or whiplash or asthma or male sexual reluctance, try switching to Shiatsu's finger-pressure massage. Or bioenergetic exercises. If you're ticklish, go back to golf. Or Viagra.

And there's always massage, which isn't dirty. Unless it's in a parlor. If it takes place at the YMCA or in a clean and orderly studio, it's okay, especially if the practitioner is clothed in natural fibers or serves alfalfa tea. She should look unsubtly countercultural.

The "Others"

I recall spending a weekend at a small inn in California where I stumbled into a room of naked glistening bodies and a couple of massage tables about which clustered beaming acolytes of the new belief. At the time, I had no idea of the significance of my find. Now I know I was in a tiny spiritual community, a suburb of California's coastal 1883 utopia, Paradiso. There were classes taking place; the question was, what kind?

My instincts shut it out. Even now I cringe as I educate myself about alternate faiths—a reflex against "other" contamination, such as body resurrection.

Reich Is Release

At an age when my market value has plummeted, I feel like my pregnancy-seeking friend's husband whose sperm count read six, not sixty. I tell myself that what's blocked is not my sexual energy; it's men's eyes! Am I to find release in Reichian therapy's orgonic wet dreams? Reich, called the father of holistic health and vital force, taught Ida Rolf.

For further manipulation, see an expert in applied kinesiology. That should tingle your spinal nerves. There are thirty-one pairs to choose from, all awaiting you like beauty pageant contestants. Then there are the neo-Reichians, Aston patterners and rebirthers, Touch for Health proselytizers, Jin Shin Do-ers, yoga teachers, laughter and dance and movement and Gestalt therapists and neonatalists, New Age physicists, orthomolecular medics, and an entire pantheon of spiritual growth freaks and psychic healers.

You wonder why I yearn to take up golf?

A Confession

I have a problem with the laying on of hands. Can I admit that although I adore spas, I hate massage? I don't like to be touched by outsiders, and I don't need past-life regression to remember why. I hate being kneaded like a mound of dough. Bruises don't attract me. If someone pounded me, I'd feel like beating them up. Or I'd bite off their ear like Mike Tyson did. I once described myself as the most violent pacifist in America.

Golf and Guilt

Will golf help? I like the idea of smacking that little ball, of pounding it instead of me. That isn't New Age. New Age blames nothing on the club or ball; it takes the guilt onto itself. If I break a leg on the links, New Agers would say I have myself to blame. It's not a question of the wrong shoes or indigestion. I picked those shoes to trip in. And how have I reordered my nutrition? Have I eliminated meat, cigarettes, alcohol, drugs, sugar, eggs, and salt? Have I worked out the sins of past lives? Am I still bathing in the rendered animal fat of guilt? Another point about meat: silverback gorillas do not eat it. Triple the size of a man, with thirty times his strength, they're voracious fruit consumers. Even the Texas steers we eat gobble up grain and grass.

By comparison, golf looks simple. Instead of traversing the concrete of bodywork studios, there's plenty of grass. If you don't feel like *shlepping* from hole to hole, you can cop out by lying down on the thick turf. Besides, there aren't millennia of sins to confront. There's just a little ball. You whack at it; either it goes in the hole or it doesn't. If you play alone (a no-no in New Age *communitas*), you have the same advantage as in solitaire: you can cheat all you like. To reduce frustration and cut down on stress, you can—assuming that nobody's looking—drop the ball in the hole yourself if it doesn't get the message. Even if you lose it in the rough, it's not a loss. There are lots of balls where that one came from. And remember, you will have had a good walk. Don't believe the guy who says that golf is a good walk spoiled.

Golf Is Sublime

Golf—not that you'd compare ball dropping with rolfing or orgonic sex—is sublime. Spiritual? No, but it evens the score. It's another point for mainstream. An authoritarian vote for supermarket versus agrarian, accredited versus alternative, institutional versus anarchic, empirical mystical healing versus AMA pathology, assault weapons versus peace. Are we going to let these Aquarian weirdoes overcome us? Co-opt them! Kidnap their shamans. Tie up their spirit guides. Steal their genes. Stuff your colon. Bathe in ice cream. Hoard and masturbate with golf balls.

The Gray Panthers will support you. If they don't, I will.

Chapter Twelve

Death and Dying

Do We Have To?

Five Steps to Nirvana

To the superstitious, omens of death may include broken mirrors, the scent of flowers, unfamiliar noises, dreams, and visions.

Must I die before I wake? And pray the Lord my soul to take? A New Age *Handbook on Death and Dying* by Carol Parrish-Harra hauls out the old Christian homilies along with salt-and-pepper grains on the *kabbala*, *The Egyptian Book of the Dead*, the Hindu Vedas, and Elisabeth Kübler-Ross's five steps to dying. To repeat her mantra: denial, anger, bargaining, preparatory depression, and acceptance. The last step fades into a rosy glow as spirit guides, angels, "beings of light and love," or whatever name these celestial beings are known by, triumph.

Here Parrish-Harra shares her near-death and out-of-body experiences. She also takes us through the deaths of two infant sons and an automobile collision that killed her daughter and grandchild. The accident account that ends the text is accompanied by copies of newspaper articles that document the deaths. As if this stream of tragedies were not gruesome enough—is the author trying to convince us, and herself, that

85

the accident happened?—when I came to these pages, a small photo of a smiling girl fell out. Was this the daughter (too young) or the grandchild (too old) or the work of a reader who had lost her own? Or of a spirit guide who could not resist tampering with what should be left alone?

Like other death texts, this one attempts to justify as well as explain such mysteries as the visitation of ghosts of the recently deceased to their former precincts. My hunch is that familiarity with the dead's image might cause this phenomenon so often attributed to a material manifestation of the immaterial.

Mother, Please Go Back to Your Own Bed

As my mother lay dying after surgery, I felt and heard her ghost on the staircase in her house and spent hours sitting bolt-upright in abject terror lest the spirit of her death attempt to occupy her bed. The next morning I sat by her bedside to hear her, semiconscious, describe her near-death experience. As for my father, the night he died I thought I saw him trying to reenter our home.

In folktales and legends, seeing your own wraith is a sign that you are expiring. Wraiths of the dying appear to their children, arriving to take one last look. Wraiths may also signal a catastrophe or give news of an impending death in the family. Mom and Pop are good ghosts who, offering protection and love, should be differentiated from the evil revenants who hang about their former premises or return to cause trouble. Terror of my own impending death is reflected in the horror I felt when each dying parent attempted to back out of the contaminated realm and into their former home.

Jews returning from the cemetery to eat and reminisce wash their hands outside the abode of the deceased. We who perform this act of absolution throw a handful of soil over the casket as it is lowered into the grave: *Dust to dust* . . . Washing, we cleanse ourselves of death's corruption.

Sometimes the living *seek out* the dead. Missing a loved one, they strive to make contact through a medium or spiritualist at a seance.

Delving into the supernatural may make us queasy or defensive. In crossing the line are we usurping the power of God?

Me and Parrish-Harra

As I read the work of Carol Parrish-Harra, I saw Dad, the tired fat man, returning from an ordinary day at work, shoulders hunched, breathing hard, head cast down, brow-beaten. He returned in death as in life—no blare of trumpets, no triumph. But I am not a Christian healer like Parrish-Harra, whose claims to New Age wisdom were learned while providing for the bereaved, being a support person, and helping families, along with the dying, to cope.

Shiva Means We're with Ya

Orthodox Jews in Boston, like Muslims in northwest China's Ürümqi, sit in mourning (shiva) seven days. Rituals to assuage the restless recent dead pervade other religions as well. In Egypt and Tibet, proscriptions deal with those who have crossed over. According to the *Kabbala,* souls seek bodies through which they may return to earth.

In the Far East, the living are ruled by "hungry ghosts." For years after a death, paper money is flung on the grave, and bonfires are lit on the nearest mountain to guide ancestors to their homes, where a feast is set lest family members—and they themselves—forget.

Back to New Age

The current vernacular is infused with terms like "support person" and "near-death experience." We capitalize "Death Is Life, Too" and "Beauty Lives" so that we may be heard.

Having heard, someone believes Parrish-Harra's claim to New Ageism. On the acknowledgments page of her book, this unknown has inked, in bold script: "New Age is full of lies—it will kill you. Only Jesus is the way to the Living God." But this anonymous Fundamentalist will not have the last word. Below his inscription another has written, in a tighter script, "Keep your opinions to yourself."

New Age is as threatening as death, as all that's new is to those who cleave to the old. The perceived menace in Jesus' rise to notoriety as the messenger of a new age brought him to the crucifix at age thirty-three.

What Happened to Eden

If an article in *Time* magazine is to be believed, Eden is Old Age. Reproduced in full-color is a section of Giotto's masterpiece, *The Ascension*. Here the Messiah, accompanied by angelic hosts, is called heavenward while Mary, robed in cobalt blue like the sky, prays below with the saintly apostles. A poll is quoted, in which 61 percent of those surveyed (religious persuasion unknown) believe that after death they will go directly to heaven.

As for the 39 percent of us who are not so sure, are we speeding straight to hell or will our unresurrected bones waste away in purgatory? Will we take our bones with us or leave them to molder to dust? If I am heading to the New Jerusalem, I hope it's less quarrelsome than the Old.

Where's There?

Where, after all, is heaven? Here I am asking New Age questions about the oldest space there is. Is it like the Internet, where space may be virtual, or like the isles of the blessed—the Elysian Fields, an essence of "neither earth, air, fire, nor water" surrounding the outermost of nine nested spheres?[1] All this is to be anticipated, like ice in a drought, or Billy Graham's driving "down the golden streets in a yellow Cadillac." Jeffrey Burton Russell, a pundit on Satan, describes heaven as reality itself.[2]

New Age is impatient. It demands instant gratification and relief not only in the hereafter but in the *now*. The double throne of jasper is the massage table where white-robed elders await their certificates to practice what is preached. There do not seem to be fluttering angels, wings, or clouds. But then, I am wary of visions and have had enough of repentance.

Although at times anarchic, New Age is anything but atheistic. It stirs a melting pot, a vegetarian brew of Judeo-Christian, Native American,

Hindu, and Buddhist beliefs while aspiring to Nirvana. Nirvana is non-being, way beyond pearly gates, beyond the creation-destruction dance of Shiva, beyond the Pure Land and jeweled palaces of the Buddha Amitabha. Nirvana is beyond New Age, beyond the matrilineal goddess, beyond the restorative aroma of mama's chicken soup.

Part Three

Down to Earth

Chapter Thirteen

Hostel Shmostel

The Great Education Bake-Off of Senior Camp

The Package Tour Repackaged

Years ago I explored the possible connection between travel and education. I tried writing off a trip to Italy—"to study art independently"—as a tax-deductible expense. The result? I got audited, and had the temerity to show up for my first IRS "interview" in red, white, and blue Italian shoes and an ankle-length mink coat. The IRS agent, a dowdy spinster in a mildewed black dress, didn't take to this flamboyance at all. Nor did she find amusing my lack of documentation for claimed expenses.

Back then I could not have predicted that three decades later fellow seniors would steal and perfect my act, but perfect it through forethought. Old Age now, I still scoff at "package tours" for lazy brains and *nebbishes*.

Elderhostel has no such scruples. There the package tourist is not a *nebbish*, but an emeritish.

Emeritus Worth the Paper It's Written on

What does *emeritus* mean? The basic idea is to creep around the world in segregated buses or in planes, on senior discounts and crepe soles, to view the fountain of pain. To bus or not to bus? The alternative is Tibet, sixty kilometers from an airport with rescue helicopters. Search out the sacred truths at 12,000 feet above sea level. Create like Hemingway, confront the bulls, write your own sky burial while I sneak in and out in forty-eight hours to fool the gods of altitude. Lhasa may be the only place in the world where we dial "O" for oxygen, not operator.

While my peers are shopping for Buddha, water containers in hand like babies' bottles, I am sniffing the monastery outskirts for my Black Tara: jewelry. Coral and turquoise have me in thrall. Earrings, head or cod pieces, forehead ropes and bangles, toe rings and nose rings, rings to hide wrinkled knuckles.

The Emeritushies
(New Freedom or Old Trap?)

New Agers drink soy formulas, Old Agers skim milk? Not in Lhasa. At 12,000 feet, who can predict what the gods of altitude will do to milk. Try water. Not ordinary tap water, but mineral water free of additives and pollutants, including age. Tell this to the emeritushies.

They swarm to the Himalayas (accent on the second syl*la*ble), where they are locked into the Holiday Inn to study The Paradigm of Changing Universe. Sequestered from the mountains and skies, they seek enlightenment in an elder kiddie camp, their new freedom not in tampons, but on a potter's wheel or weaving loom. Trying to forget, to reshape Ulysses' desertion, Penelope's fate . . . Buddha will save them, or oat bran, or Lao-tzu. Just a short hop to China. Excuse me—Tibet *is* China. And so, too, is Hong Kong.

Elder Camps

Elderhostel caters to seniors with long-distance aspirations and short attention spans. The sojourns offered by Lifetime Learning typically last four or five nights with temptations (in Ontario) ranging from Unlock the Mysteries of Each Religion to Is There Unity in This Diversity? to Turning Rawhide and Ash into Snowshoes. Warm weather enthusiasts can head south to tackle Pirates of the Caribbean or, following the smoke from George Burns's cigar, a course called Oh, God! For agnostics there are Cinematic Insights into Religion, Humor and the Divine, Carpetbaggers and Confederates (in Georgia), or one can snorkel with the Kahaluu Bay fish at Hawaiian Village Experience in Kona.

What could be more romantic than to visit the Volcanic Art Center ("the world's most active volcano") at a military camp site where one can loll among wild orchids and tree ferns like Bob Hope and Dorothy Lamour in a road movie? Kentucky offers Celebrations of Tibetan Sacred Music and Dance amid the bluegrass, sanctioned by His Holiness the Dalai Lama, with monks from the Drepung Loseling Monastery. If multiphonic droning is not your thing, you can try The *Shtetl* to the Studio at Baltimore Hebrew University in Maryland.

While snowshoes reappear in Minnesota, Mississippi tenders Grapevine Twining, a once-in-a-lifetime opportunity to sidetrack addictive thirst into bird feeders or swans. Missouri flaunts The Human Truman and Montana Grizzlies of Yellowstone, a "controversial species" of the ecosystem. (Seniors were the "controversial species" before we were trussed and crammed into snowshoes to become politically correct trekkers.) I myself am tempted by Lust and Seduction in the Bible (New Mexico) or, more chastely, Allegory of Western Bias.

For those who demand hands-on experience in New Mexico, there is painting or potting at Pueblo to Navajo: From the Stone Age to the Atomic Age; Loom, Cradleboard and Hogan Galloping (through Gallup?); and Folsom cavemen hunting saber-toothed tigers or eating giant sloths.

Romance in Elder Camp

By this time, we might all agree that there are many options to TV sitcoms and nursing homes. And we have not even left the continental borders of the United States.

Why do we seniors need this postdoc education? Surely, not to get a job. Or to make more money. Romance? Perhaps. But that's no more likely than bumping baskets in a supermarket to become attached. We need to collect our New Age beads to purchase not love, but credibility.

Old Age Has No Brochures

New Age has a future in dazzling brochures, untrodden shores, and, in peek-a-boo coves, an oyster eating its own pearl. Old Age has maybe a faded postcard from the nursing home or the Hemlock Society, the script obscene as an Atlantic City postcard showing not the hotel where WASPs stayed (Jews stayed in rooming houses on streets named for the forty-eight Union states), but an outhouse and the leering creep who ran the burlesque shows featuring Abbott and Costello, or Laurel and Hardy (once described as a violin string and bow). Before low-cal diets, they knew what the score was. Who needed to be an Einstein? None went beyond the eighth grade. Could you eat an education? Some did.

Elder Groupies

The emeritushies are New Age. They're all in elderhostel grad school. They come home to frame certificates and call up folks they spent a week saying goodbye to—those on the right track for two weeks, or in Nirvana for ten days. Groupies on the edge.

Am I doomed to become an elder groupie convinced that, sure as the sun rises, breakfast ends not at Tiffany's, but in a Quonset hut whose lone water tap dribbles like a ninety-year-old penis? Is *this* all there is, some godforsaken plain outside a Mongolian yurt whose "shared bath" is a feces-clogged shed where the local girls smile into cracked glass to smear on their made-in-Taiwan lipsticks? Such scenes never make the brochures.

For New Age trekkers or *shleppers*, being outfitted with a backpack is like being laced into baby's first shoes. Elder groupies bear their packs like Jesus did his cross—a sign of membership, of true faith, of belonging. The packing of the sack separates the true believers from the half-committed. Never mind that there are shops along the trail, the true believer packs as if her life depended on it. And it does if she's not to cross the line to the other side. The believer hovers near the line she will not cross. Each geegaw she packs is key to an eternity half-hidden by incipient cataracts.

The Preparation Fetish

The preparation fetish isn't confined to Geritol-agers. When my sister died in her forties (wincing at a sun that wouldn't shine), she left behind numerous satin cases stuffed with every sort of wash and dry, emollient, colorant, analgesic, Lifesaver, gum, and extra eyeglass case. Death caught her unawares, swooping down like an eagle from a mountain she was too nearsighted to see. Unprepared, the poor goose had done nothing but pack for dry lips, sore eyes, runny stomach, and itchy vagina, her valises crammed for every conceivable disaster except the clutch of the swift-swooping reaper.

The New Ager will never be found unprepared. Panaceas do not fill her drawers and closets; they are strapped to her spine like a hunchback's sack. The pack will no sooner let go of her—nor she of it—than a Siamese twin would release his mate.

Bags and Cancer

On the street where my mother lived was an ordinary woman famous for one thing: her Frigidaire. On a lower-middle-class street where everyone's refrigerator was crammed full with necessities to stave off the hunger of "the starving children of Poland"—stuffed so full that it was nearly impossible to shut the door—this woman's box was stuffed with paper and empty plastic bags. She was so fearful of running out of bags to put things in that she left no room for the food they were meant to hold.

The woman developed cancer and held on for years—to the bags *and* the cancer. To her credit, she wouldn't let go, perhaps because of the house in which she, and my mother across the street, lived. For mutual protection, these houses were joined at the lip, neck, and hip. Row houses, they're called. They held on to each other in clans that stretched a full block, and so they had no lateral light, just fore and aft. There, insulated against doom, big black beetles entered every house like Axis tanks through crevices invisible to the naked eye.

Then the bag lady—which is what we called her, though she lived in a tight ship of a house, unlike her homeless namesakes who came after-ward—died. When I heard that, I wondered what they did, not with her, which was foretold, but with the bags, the empty sandless bags stowed against flood, miscarriage, tornado, lightning, rape, ungrateful children, dust, carbuncles, divorce, and world war.

But that was Old Age.

Home Alone

Just as the elderhostel New Ager is married to her pack of safeguards, so she clamps on to her group. New Age is composed of groupies—trekkers and climbers all. Lone strollers like me have no clout.

New Age groupies have explored every cave from Guangzhou to Timbuktu, gasping and posing with the hanging bats and screeching monkeys of Indonesia, the donkeys about to carry them up the white cliffs of Santorini, or the yaks of Pakistan, or the Gobi camels, or the ele-phants of Delhi. New Age is leisure class. These folks will not go darkly into that dreaded night, though they will without qualm enter the novice tunnel from Dover to Paree.

The Fountain of Youth

New Age has conquered the Appalachian Trail north to lobster pot Maine. Our wrinkled-apple knees argue with the smooth pears of youth.

Gasping and drooling, we clutch at each other, wave at TV cameras. It's taken only five years and we're halfway through!

Time doesn't run out on New Age as it does on Old Age. Or if it does, New Age is racing ahead too fast to notice. Its martyrs drop on the trail—no shuffling off to Buffalo. Narrow-gauge railroads are nearly dead; buses, desegregated. But helicopters make periodic trips in to clean up those sacrificed to the turtle-throated lamas of Gigatse.

In the New Age we all drink out of the same fountain. It is deeply polluted, and its name is not Youth.

Chapter Fourteen

Virtual Reality

The Real

Conversion experiences do not occur only while fasting or on a massage table at Big Sur. They can also occur in cyberspace while gripping handlebars and wearing lightweight goggles connected by wire to a computer. A creepy creature limb called an ARM gives us the power to reach out and maneuver illusory 3-D objects. If you push the molecular images, they may push back. These are illusory. Or are *we?*

According to Howard Rheingold, author of *Virtual Reality* and editor of *Whole Earth Review,* you can enter the virtual reality (VR) of cyberspace through a computer called a "reality engine." And where *is* cyberspace? Rheingold describes his launch into this realm in these words: "A headpiece . . . covered my face, and a three-dimensional binocular television filled my field of view with electronic mirages. . . . My body wasn't in the computer world I could see around me, but one of my hands accompanied my point of view onto the vast electronic plain that seemed to surround me, replacing the crowded laboratory I had left behind, where my body groped and probed. . . . A sensor-webbed glove synched my physical gestures in the room where my body was located to the movements of a cartoonlike glove that floated in the computer-created world."[1]

A Form of Tripping

No wonder my mother clung to the neighborhood and never ventured downtown. Going downtown then was akin to stepping through the dimensional doorway of telepresence today. "Telepresence," Rheingold tells us, "is a form of out-of-the-body experience . . . the name of a concept, a tool, an experience. It might also be one of the names for the way VR is changing what it means to be human."[2]

MIT's Artificial Intelligence Laboratory, under the direction of Martin Minsky and John McCarthy, coined the term "artificial intelligence." Minsky's modest goal was to simulate human thought through thinking machines capable of convincing human users that they were present in a remote location.

Is this a form of tripping? Yes, as is the creation of robots that feel and work like our own hands. Human perceptions and reactions may someday be linked to these remote semiautonomous robots. If they are, we could then be our own space robots, feeling that we are in a different place than we really are. Is it any wonder that Tsukuba City, home to such research, has the highest suicide rate in Japan?

Researchers have also been working on robotic artificial guide dogs for the blind, to be operated by remote control. Such robots, known as MELDOGS, are described as partially intelligent. Our conceit should be tempered by a computer's recent victory over the reigning world chess champion. While computers are given the edge in evaluating computations, storing massive amounts of data, and remembering it all, humans are far ahead in pattern recognition, evaluation, and context.

Is This Me Here or Am I over There?

The sense of physical presence is the sine qua non of virtual reality. Feeling out of it? Rest assured that virtual environments do require human interfacing. "The human part of a teleoperator partnership provides the cognitive-perceptual expertise," Rheingold informs us.[3] The idea is for humans to not only adapt to but also *become* machines. Rheingold describes the synchronicity between the robot's movements he controlled and his own moves as an out-of-body experience. Strapped into a "dentist's chair" and to a head-mounted display, he felt he was "here" while at the same time standing over "there."

Why? Because this tele-existence system "allows an operator to use robots' ultrasonic, infrared and other, otherwise invisible, sensory information with the computer-graphics–generated pseudorealistic sensation of presence."[4]

The MELDOGS and Me

Aside from MELDOGS for the blind and robot slaves for quadriplegics, how do we steer our arthritic joints through telepresence? I've no desire to command flocks of remote robots or to probe molecules with my fingers. Skeptically, I'm waiting for sex-at-a-distance devices. Aren't these already operating in bad relationships?

I think I'm having simulator sickness from keeping up with me and my double. I'll never be the impervious robot that scientists dream of, or the ideal candidate for prosthetic design. I can't deal with being neither here nor there. Ugh, I sense motion sickness coming on.

Seeing Double Is Bad Enough

As bad as it is to see double, feeling it could be worse. Yet that's what the cyber freaks would have us do. "We might soon see the day when CAD designers can not only stick their head into their designs, but reach their hands in and feel objects," Rheingold warns us.[5] So much for cybersex. This could lead to lawsuits over harassment. Was he or was he not present at the remote hazardous site? Is this what is meant by a "telepresence *test-bed*"?

Components of telepresence might include "a glove in a garage north of London, a teleoperator setup in Culham, a small mobile vehicle laboratory in Manchester."[6] These read like body parts of a cybermurder.

Touching through a Joystick

We're not done with sex. Stirring a virtual substance—ice cubes in molasses, for instance—feels real, if somewhat kinky. This simulated feel of reality is known as virtual tactility. How about virtual gonorrhea? Or virtual pregnancy? Are these mere haptic illusions? What is sex without texture? The compliant skin comes in contact with an object . . .

Run your joystick over sandpaper. If that doesn't turn you on, write your name on broken glass—an alternate for tattooing. In the event that the joystick doesn't work, try a glove or grip or fingertip buzzer. The truth is that haptic simulation might be thought of as faking orgasm.

Telemanipulation

We refer to the instrumental gesture. Allegedly, the modular feedback keyboard allows you to feel the virtual violin and other instruments. The keyboard is actually (virtually?) a violin bow that looks like a keyboard, with attached stainless steel finger loops. See how far we have moved from "a spade is a spade"? But then, a spade is Old Age whereas the keyboard took twelve years of New Age tinkering. Research proceeds by synthesizing not only sound but also the instrument.

Chapter Homework

1. Make a molecule you can feel in your hand.
2. Try to design a gestural traducer—a way of turning human gesture into computer data.
3. Create a language for connecting gestures to sounds and images.
4. Manipulate graphic forms in real time. Try this in virtual time.
5. Give a virtual violin and bow to a nonvirtual (real) violinist.
6. Attempt to create a virtual violin that can do what a real violin can't do.
7. Try finding a missing kid in a cybermall.
8. If you fail at numbers 1 through 7, please don't cop out into virtual warfare. New Age means peace.

How are you going to keep the cybernerds down on the farm after they've tasted VR?

Chapter Fifteen

Networking

Lowering the Hierarchies

Holistic health is a social entity. Forget hierarchical structures—decentralize, de-capitalize, de-stress.

You may have been around in the '60s and '70s for the conscious-ness-raising, civil rights, women's rights, human rights, and human potential movements. The '90 are alive with community action, consumer rights, patient rights, children's rights, senior rights, animal rights, black rights, Hispanic rights, Asian rights, employee and employer rights, undocumented alien rights, and documented alien rights.

Down with authoritarian; up with egalitarian nativist grassroots. Feel the "French fried fingers" of Jin Shin Do. Revelation is modeled on cata-strophe theory, the ecstatic leap of a system following a set of gradually changing circumstances.

The Networking Mensches

A *mensch* is a guy who's above average. When Esalen, temple of the human potential movement, was founded above the crashing waves of Big

Sur, it was referred to by a Bay Area leader as an "aristocracy of those who care." The movement took its name from "Human Potentialities"—title of a lecture series given by Aldous Huxley in 1962. With the creation of Esalen, California came to be taken seriously by transplanted Easterners like myself.

When I moved there in 1978, I sought to change my cellular chemistry rather than my mind-set. I was running from familial East Coast cancer. After years of psychotherapy, I felt armed to live as a grown-up. While my daughter rushed off to Esalen, I shunned networks for social change, seeing them as quasi-religious cults that stressed mind control, mindless obedience, and love slathered with quasi-religious blather. Mutual help networks were agencies for group masturbation.

Could Gandhi's "grouping entities"—the collective body-mind—transform society or would I be left in the ash of the conflagration? There are those who say fire may be avoidable through more harmony between us and the earth, sky, wind, and water.

A Paradigm Shift

New Age signifies the power of an aligned minority to instigate and speed up a paradigm shift. Don't belittle the influence of the feminist movement. In the words of a Chinese proverb, Women hold up half the sky. I know it's true even if some days I'm too tired to join them or too busy looking over my shoulder to see who's holding up the other half.

Doubts multiply like gnats on rotting fruit. Will transformation truly lead to transcendence? J. A. English-Lueck lists three types of available New Age structures: egalitarian (peer networks of holistic practitioners and workshops), authoritarian (religious and theurgic associations, as well as residential communities, including *kibbutzim,* under charismatic leaders), and institutional (professional associations).[1]

Robert Ellwood's "protean man" reminds us that from discontent and discord comes spiritual life untied to cultural identity. Identity itself is changing amid decentralized networks. The emerging empirical tradition in healing is reminiscent of the role shamans have played as religious leaders in their cultures.

The Modern Age May Be Kaput

If the modern age is finished, what follows? Will loners like me, independent wise-guy girls and geeks, be willing to reach out? Will I link up with a co-op if it means co-opting my independence? Having left the lotus land of California, will I join a New Age snob club? If cyberspace is elusive, where does a mouthy heretic go when she's not a mystic (from the Greek *mythos,* meaning to keep silent)?

Familial alienation versus Reichian self-responsibility. Isolation versus the Institute for Structural Integration. A dark, solitary cell versus the Emissaries of Divine Light.

Light May Come with Religious Baggage

The light following the end of the modern age is apt to carry religious overtones, whether it shines apocalyptically with the second coming of Christ or merely with the appearance of a raccoon spirit guide. As for names, the Church of Religious Science seems to cover all bases.

Spiritual goals impact on social transformation. In his remarkable examination titled *The Devils of Loudon,* Aldous Huxley referred to the phenomenon of *horizontal self-transcendence,* a means of escaping from the "horrors of insulated selfhood" by associating with a cause more embracing than one's immediate interests. Without horizontal self-transcendence, he said, there would be no art, science, law, philosophy, or even civilization; nor would there be war, systematic intolerance, or persecution. He added: "How can we have the good without the evil. . . ? The answer is that we cannot have it so long as our self-transcendence remains merely horizontal. . . . If this self-identification with what is human is not accompanied by a conscious and consistent effort to achieve upward self-transcendence into the universal life of the Spirit, the goods achieved will always be mingled with counterbalancing evils."[2] Huxley went on to quote the French philosopher Blaise Pascal: "Truth without charity is not God."[3]

One difficulty with cult desires to achieve upward self-transcendence is the impulse to convert others. Like the exorcists and priests surrounding the possessed nuns and prioress in Huxley's seventeenth-century morality lesson, New Agers are zealous in their conversions. In health food emporiums known as Whole Earth and Alfalfa's and Wild Oats, cyberspace cafés, photocopy marts, and post offices, they sow their seeds, their eager voices preaching the wonders of cell transformation, bodywork, and meditation. They are attractive, healthy looking, zealous-eyed.

The Spiritual Revolution

Is terrorism a factor? In an essay published in *Urban Terrorism,* Robin Wright, Ronald R. Ostrow, and Marlene Cimons, citing bombings of the World Trade Center in New York and the Federal Building in Oklahoma City, examine the awakening of Americans to our lack of immunity to attack. They contend that our tradition of liberty prevents us from responding with stricter security measures.

In the same text Adam Gopnick refers to the cultural history of Wild West violence while Sharon Begley discusses the threat of nuclear stockpiles. Thomas Powers, disputing Gopnick's assumption that terrorism has been effective, writes of improvements in detection intelligence and technologies that are making terrorism less lethal.[4]

New Age Is Anti

Has the terror of terrorism inspired us to look for new or old ways of coping with stress? New Age is antiviolent, antiwar, anticontamination of ourselves and our environment. I can't believe that meditation, Reichian orgonics, or bodywork will stop terrorism. Belief in mysticism and psychic powers can act as a substitute for organized religion—a cathedral into which the fearful soul can retreat for refuge, for membership in an intuitive elite where we can feel not only safe but superior to the unenlightened.

I remember the contempt in a roommate's eyes when she saw me take sugar instead of honey. Honey as an antidote to chaos? On with the new world order! Which is precisely what terrorists believe *they* are creating.

Chapter Sixteen

Our Sacred Land

The Rape of Pele

While roving with guides and gurus, we have not yet looked down at our feet dug into allegedly sacred land. Spaces for spiritual reflection may have either a communal or a solitary focus, and may be graced either with or without a gifted leader. Locations include mountains; sites for gods and religious ascents; tombs or buildings containing relics, or marking the scene of miracles or sacrifices; and places of assembly.

In Hawaii land incarnates such living deities as the volcano goddess Pele. According to a printed advertisement: "The Hawaiian religion, which thousands of us still observe, is different from Christianity or Judaism or Buddhism. Like Native Americans, our religion is in nature. . . . On the Big Island of Hawaii, the goddess Pele appears to us daily in all her forms. . . . For us it is a sacrilege for an energy company to come along and drill holes in Pele's body, to capture her steam for geothermal power, to destroy her rain forests, all so a few people can make money."[1]

Hawaiians have also protested use of the sacred island of Kahoolawe for United States bombing practice. Here in New Mexico, Native Americans struggle against constant threats of usurping their land for extensions of ski basin parking lots, Anglo housing developments, and mineral grabs. It is no wonder that Amazon Indians call whites the "termite people."

Arable Land Is Dwindling

In the face of an exploding global population, where resources need to be conserved to feed, house, support, and protect, land is sacred. Attuned to waste, exploitation, and wanton destruction of fresh water, forests, and agricultural acreage, New Age has mobilized to publicize and, where possible, tackle these concerns forthrightly.

For most Americans "land is a dead thing," says Shoshone Indian Joe Sanchez. "When our elders try to explain that Indian people die if they are removed from the land, Americans don't know what they're talking about."[2] In the words of Hopi elder John Lansa, "This is the spiritual center of this land . . . right here on this mesa. . . . In those [old] days the air was clear and everyone could see far. We always looked to the Earth Mother for food and nourishment. We never took more than we needed. . . . When the white men came, everything started to get out of balance."[3]

War against Christ and Crone

As Barbara Walker points out, American Indians saw land and human as one, and God as part of the earth he created rather than, as Anglo Christians saw him, outside it. "They believed the mother would provide sufficient nourishment for the needs of every creature, provided her gifts were never abused by human greed. . . . Conservation of resources was an essential part of a religion largely shaped by women."[4] Walker compares the patriarchal tendency to compartmentalize man and nature with the crone's belief in recycling.

To American Indians, land *is* life. Jerry Mander tells of an Onandaga crone who stood firm in refusing a big cash offer from a power company that hoped to put power lines along a right-of-way across the reservation. The old woman said, "Not one more foot, ever"—a point on which there was unanimous tribal agreement.[5]

Earth externalized the goddess. "Whatever references to the primal Goddess couldn't be diabolized, masculinized or quietly dropped," says Walker, "early churchmen tended to convert into mythical saints."[6]

New Age feminists have converted the ancient goddess to a latter-day saint. Women's studies are obsessed with recovering the Wise One—whether Mother Earth, Queen of Heaven, or the Diamond Sow of Southeast Asia—and restoring her to the cracked dais from which she was pulled by mother-hating sons. Thus, the chants and ceremonials, the open-air festivals and academic rituals, attributing to goddess intuition the superior intelligence of experience and analysis.

Promising Eve a Rose Garden

Take Back the Night is the name of an annual march in San Francisco to protest violence against women. Even among the most virile misogynists, while males are spitting blood at their lack of a womb, earth is perceived as a woman. Witness the Promise Seekers, who use feminist tactics to grab whatever droplets of semen have spilled from their holy grail. After centuries of persecuting women, mutilating and murdering their own progeny, they promise to fulfill their duties as fathers, husbands, lovers, and sons. Will they promise to stop dropping nuclear bombs and chemical weapons, wiping out their own race and the sustainable soil faster than they can procreate? Matriarchal morality did not annihilate; it conserved.

Mother Earth Is a Guy

Other New Age men dress up in women's clothing—not because they are gay, but because, like Greek actors who strapped on phalluses, they hook on the yoni to affirm their female souls. A male poet, father of three, storms a woman's meeting at a writers' conference to announce that he is as much woman as us.

These self-feminizing guys have got to have it all. Having the power is not enough; they need to play at being victimized, at being not only god but goddess, Eddie as Erda and Ertha, the true muse of *Der Ring des Nibelungen*.

New Age Is a Guilt Trip

New Age white men and women yearn to expiate their guilt. They seek to atone for the pillage left after their (and their ancestors') plunder of natural resources. In the process, they strive to take the last resource the Indian has by getting into his brain and becoming him through imitation of ritual, healing, and hallucinogenic procedures—consummating the final digestion of god and man. They eliminate the need for balance by *becoming* the balance.

Some call this past-life clearing, a journey into the soul. Whose soul? Anyone's, as long as I don't have to deal with mine. Off I'll go to Mexico or India or Tibet to feel the ancient (now new) vibes.

Or Stay at Home

Conceive of a Civitate Dei, a New Jerusalem, taking its guidelines from the dean of arcology, visionary architect Paolo Soleri, who tells us how to plant our very own raspberry patch in the utopian landscape. The New Jerusalem, he says, is "holistic—in the direction of the spirit, part of the asentropic pull away from the pollution of entropy."[7]

Stop! I need a semantics cop.

Soleri shrugs his shoulders. How can one escape from this tautological merry-go-round? "Abstract utopia with its map of despair," he tells us, "is the only other alternative."[8] Translation: Raspberries alone may not guarantee utopia.

Sacred Spaces

If raspberry patches do not suffice, domestic priestess Martha Stewart suggests building your own window boxes labeled (courtesy of Soleri) Truly Sacred Space, a spot "infinitesimally closer to the Omega God which life is intent on creating."[9] Sacred spots have also been defined as "spaces in man's environment where the mind is stimulated to focus on spiritual thought; and where this occurs in communion with others, rather than alone."[10]

There is sacral space as well, greeted with hosannas from New Age muses warped by Buddhist and Hindu seers. According to an unidentified seer, we should consider *akasha*, the space of the heart where externals cannot be assessed quantitatively. Although such external places as temples and sacred mountains may be important jumping-off points for our journey within, we are told they must never be confused with sacred space itself.

Now we are approaching the *real* that always *is*. The real, in New Age vernacular, is the immediate moment and the I AM experience. In a flash we sense who we are; to use the Hindu phrase, we have "crossed the river."

I Am the Only One Left on the Bank

I, whose eyes have seen Varanasi as well as the Western Wall and Dome of the Rock, am still stuck in AM I, when New Agers are luffing smugly with Sufi mystics and Zen priests to I AM. The words of Kabir, fourteenth-century pilgrim and weaver saint, echo in my ears. When asked where he could lie down to rest so that his feet would not face rudely toward the Kaaba in Mecca, he replied, "Is there any place where the All-Holy is not present?"

The notion that land is sacred predates automobile pollution and urban and tenement overcrowding. American Indians, Indian subcontinent Hindus and Buddhists, Chinese sages and Japanese priests and Greek pharmacologists have all made obeisance to the land, using it and its produce for healing.

Whatever Happened to "Fresh" Air?

While working on attitudinal healing and polarity therapy, how do we heal the planet we depend on to support our breath? One book states that each day the United States alone produces 700,000 tons of toxic waste.[11] That's 250 million tons a year! According to a reviewer, "Six trillion pounds of chemicals are produced annually for plastics, glues, fuels, dyes and other chemical products that all find their way into the environment."[12] Four of these chemicals deemed safe by chemical voodooists are alleged killers; this witch's brew includes formaldehyde, the weed controls alachlor and atrazine, and the degreaser perchloroethylene, used in dry cleaning. If we are all walking chemical time-bombs, we might as well duck under the plastic bags our dry cleaners supply.

And what if the nuclear proliferation the army admits to—fifty years after the fact—*was* sent downwind during atomic bomb testing in the '50s? After investigating the deformed sheep and cows, we should examine our thyroids for cancer. (Charts for self-diagnosis have appeared in the tabloids.)

Who's Sick—the Great All-Mother or Us?

According to Tantric and Egyptian lore, goddess worship was prevalent when women were acknowledged healers. At the time, they were also inventors of alphabets, astronomers and scientists, makers of music and calendars. Women "embodied the earth and owned the real estate, as well as holding within themselves the 'wise blood' that formed life in the matrilineal clan system."[13]

Whatever happened to this alleged health of the land? If the land is sick, then so are we. As a Roswell dispatch proclaims, "I Have Seen the Alien and It Is Us."[14]

It will take more than courses in Native American spirituality, ayurveda, pranayama, and postnatal yoga to dispel the trauma. Yet if we can't heal the spirit in the land, I suppose we must work on ourselves, change behavior patterns and mind structures, and clear the way to a mindlessly joyful, if diseased, self while continuing to make the land untenable for Shakespeare's Prince Hal posing as Hecate.

Living Lightly on the Earth

Soft Touch

A soft touch is advised by environmental groups that promote stewardship rather than exploitation of natural resources. Try balance between use and domination, institutionalized medicine and personal responsibility. As power balances are readjusted, groups will "rechannel economic power by boycotts, barter, cooperative buying and business practices," says Marilyn Ferguson.[1]

I, for one, am too heavy-handed. My mother called me a klutz, inferring that I was clumsy. If anything was in my path, I bumped into it. I grew up feeling like an elephant—another term she used, even though I was thin enough to be anemic. Her critiques conditioned me to think of myself as a heavy-metal presence.

I spent years apologizing, and still have a hard time stopping. *Excuse me for spraying Jean Naté on my skin in the locker room.* (A young asthmatic is screaming that she is about to stop breathing.) *Excuse me for years of hair spray, underarm spray, perfume spray, bug spray . . .* Why can't I be like my friend H. who, covered with bites, is being driven from home and garden by gnats she refuses to spray?

Try Feng Shui

The newest cures turn out to be the oldest. Ancient Chinese wisdom cautions us to use the divination arts in assessing how to live more lightly and luckily on the planet. Feng shui, among the most revered of these arts, was practiced prior to the unification of China by the first emperor, Shi Huang di. Described as both an art and science, it has become the hottest fad in New Age architecture and design. According to its advocates, feng shui requires no more than a geomancer's compass and an act of faith.

How can this term light up a New Ager's eyes when I find its description by an adept nearly incomprehensible? In practicing feng shui you have to balance "the workings of the five elements, the movement of the Nine Palaces, the intricate relationships of *Yin* and *Yang*, and the general form of the landscape."[2] The purpose: to manipulate wind and water (*feng* and *shui*), to use the energies of heaven and earth to channel in nourishing (moving) forces and avoid destructive ones.

Design Theories and Practices

The ancient Chinese diagrammed "wheel pa-k'uas" for the "earlier and later heavens," whose eight directions correlated to fire, earth, lake, heaven, water, mountain, thunder, and wind. The pa-k'ua was derived from Tai Chi, which in turn was rooted in *wu-chi,* or the Tao. Using this knowledge of land forms and movement of the stars, you can design countermeasures to adverse conditions and contain the vapor of life (earth *ch'i*) for good purposes. This Taoist art reached its maturity during the Tang dynasty, between 618 and 960 C.E.

So far, it's easy, but that's because we haven't yet discussed the *lopan,* or geomancer's compass—which has seventeen rings to decipher and is partitioned into twenty-four directions—or the fact that land can be yang or yin, hard or soft, dynamic or still. The best feng shui sites are near mountains and water. The goal of feng shui is to locate your house, business, or temple propitiously.

The no's of feng shui sound a lot easier to decipher than the yesses, which are incestuously related in Minotaur-defying mazes. Within the house, for instance, your kitchen must not be positioned next to the garage, where incoming cars pose a danger of attack. You must not use spiral staircases which, although picturesque, enhance malevolent energy. The bedroom ceiling should not be shaped like an inverted V or it will trap negative energy. And forget the great view—picture windows "leak" energy.

Animals, Elements, and Numbers

In feng shui, land forms are named Green Dragon, White Tiger, Red Raven, and Black Tortoise, depending on their natural shapes. Pathways of concentrated energy are termed "dragon veins." Mountains are classified by shape as water, metal, earth, fire, water, or wood. These elements also interact: water nourishes and connects wood, wood enters earth and causes fire to shoot up, and certain land forms collect wind energy. Moreover, feng shui practitioners believe that big external objects like boulders, trees, dirt mounds, and sculptures can block energy to a house.

The numerology of feng shui may well come in handy. While visiting New York, I once stayed on the thirteenth floor of a hotel for two nights before a friend told me, with glee, that some months earlier the ceiling had collapsed on a couple in bed. The hotel owner was in deep trouble with the IRS. My initial thought was, "Next time I book a room in Manhattan, I'll take a geomancer's compass or a geomantic chart, or at least request a numerological consult."

As it turns out, however, such interpretations are confusing. Compare your birth date and gender with the year your house was built. What do these factors have to do with the waxing of yin and the waning of yang, the earth base or the Facing Palace or the stars of the Nine Palaces, the ruling star of the seventh or third cycle, or the numbers associated with each of these, as well as their interactions? A three-eight combination leads to suicidal death; a four-nine to success in business. If you're not good at the numbers game, watch out—you're apt to fail in business and suicide may follow.

To complicate things further, we are urged to set up more than one geomantic chart for a building, which should then be fitted onto a floor plan. If your house has gone through renovations, you might prefer to let it burn and start all over again.

Dazzle the Gullible

While memorizing certain clichés from feng shui, remember that superstition is contagious, like measles. Do you walk under ladders? Will sweeping the Karma of a building chase away poltergeists? Try it.

One thing that bothers me about this ancient wisdom is its boycott of angles, triangles, and geodesic spikes, along with such irregularities as H and L shapes, as well as houses "jailed" by pillars, stilts, and cantilevers, knocking out many of the imaginative leaps taken by Western architecture as well as builders of the Egyptian pyramids. You can see why the pharaohs might have had a hard time despite their panoply of gods. They began with a nice, simple triangular shape and cluttered it up inside with gold trinkets.

Clutter Is Old Age

Clutter is heavy. Don't clog the tight New Age spaceship. Outdated habits, thoughts, and possessions must go; following their departure, we are assured, life will be simpler. Didn't it happen at Findhorn, in the north of Scotland, and in Israel? Becoming light as bubbles, we will all express our creativity and artistry. A barren waste of sand will be transformed into a medieval tapestry.

With gazelle feet, the unicorn trips lightly over the "morass of materialism." The unicorn is a symbol of the higher self, we are told, "called from the realm of mystery to the fructification of the purified soul."[3] There she joins the Druid priestess in the forest. Together, they murmur the mantras of TM (Transcendental Meditation), vindicating humanity's expulsion from Eden, the curse of Lucifer, Mephistopheles, or Ahriman— lords of darkness who are the powers behind materialism.

Much Should Be Enough

Avaricious Arlene must give up baskets of earrings and hats and shoes, survival disguises, and costumes—to say nothing of the trinkets and trusses, the padded bras and overflowing drawers of pantyhose. She must move on serenely to Aquarian abstractions while drowning in Piscean plenitude and, dragged down by materialism, sinking like a dead fish.

She will face the Apocalypse bare-handed even as she leaves earth for the etheric mantle, surviving without the artificial fertilizers of pedicures and makeup. Will the avatar bring charge cards? As I age, I need more compost, not less!

I really do need the Logos to lift me into a supernal field when I can't cope here below. I'm still stuck on alpha when Teilhard de Chardin and his disciples are homing in on the omega point.

Autonomy

Am I willing to sink my individuality into a national self-help clearinghouse of remaindered brains? New connections are supposed to foster creativity. (My own is overfostered and undermarketed.)

The questions march like lemmings toward a shrinking sea: Am I required to be a card-carrying member of the common market? Am I ready for a local mutual-aid utopia? Does the utopian grapevine need one more sour grape?

Thirty years after the New Age was launched on the Big Sur coast, I am still a wallflower, a thorned rose on peeling wallpaper. After more than six decades, I am waiting for a guy to ask me to dance when I should be dancing with the universe.

Some days I weaken and list toward New Age. After a bout of stomach pain caused by a prescribed muscle relaxant (traditionalist medicine!) known to be dangerous for the ulcer prone, I am about to query a lady who is using a cure to "attract the right energy." She and her husband have covered their skins with magnets. In the meantime the jaw ache, diagnosed as an infection in the salivary gland, has turned out to be a diseased upper molar referring pain to my lower jaw. This must be my punishment for rejecting holistic medicine. I should "think wholeness." I must not reject the oneness of absolute being.

Millennium Itch

New Agers tells us that we are in a world crisis, at a spiritual turning point. We should pursue the All force—coffee enemas, deep tissue massage. Should I examine animal entrails too? According to the leader of a San Diego cult found dead in their bunks in matching outfits and tennies, UFOs are manned and ready. With but a few months to go until the countdown ushers in a new millennium, some simply cannot wait.

Frankly, I can. I'll stay behind with an octogenarian who says that he does not need to sleep much anymore, since the Big Sleep is coming. He does not mean the year 2000.

Still, the millennium has millions quaking. Suddenly, media attention is focused on religious persecution. Where were Christians all the years their brothers were being done in within the borders of China, Russia, Saudi Arabia, the Sudan? All of a sudden, it's news to persecute Christians.

Nor are Christians the only New Agers. I know plenty of Jews who are card-carrying members. There must be Buddhists as well, since their mantras are being used, and Hindus. I'm not sure about Muslims, who have their own niches to bow to. They would have us submit to massage five times a day. Even if I liked massage, I wouldn't take the veil in August; it's too hot then to cover one's face with a Persian carpet.

Chapter Eighteen

Sign-Off Time

Goodbye Is Easier to Say Than Hello

I once attended a recommended seminar on wills. Wills were Old Age. New Agers commissioned Loving Trust Portfolios in red leather, gold embossed. Sadly, I thought of my own mother's will that took a year to probate. I lucked out: the probate was serviced long-distance by a law school classmate of my daughter's who was doing estate work. On the phone he sounded like the perfect clone of a law school curriculum, an unemotional undertaker of the material goods left over from the burial—those remains a casket couldn't hold.

He sounded, this policeman from a P.D. James thriller, like he had "A Taste for Death."

Wills Are Old Age

Two years later and twenty-five hundred dollars poorer, clutching the binder labeled Loving Trust Portfolio, I thought sadly of the dear lady who had taken care of business as best she could. Going into the hospital for the first cancer, she'd left on the dining room table a silver bowl filled with greeting cards to be sent for graduations, birthdays, anniversaries . . .

I could have told her that wills hold up the settling of a modest estate. New Age was this thick binder, gaudy as a celebrity pet's grave at Forest Lawn. My mother would have scoffed at its size and been appalled by its price tag. Later, I found out that I could have prepared a Living Will myself for a fraction of the cost.

Arlene had not gone New Age at all. Blindly, I had followed the institutional track. At least I hadn't chickened out, as the attorney said many did, emotionally unable to appear to sign the Loving Trust Portfolio he'd prepared. It wasn't the money. Looking into the face of the dead, the daughter or son saw that it was theirs.

I Cheated

I didn't tell the attorney I'd cheated. New Age was cremation, the Neptune society. Although I'd vowed to do it that way thirty years earlier, closer to the crypt I was visualizing hellfire and brimstone, a postdeath sentient self. The only attraction—still poetic—was the scattering of my remains in an ocean.

Yet, is it New Age to add to the pollution? Flashback to a scene on the predawn Ganges: smoking pyres, women in gorgeous saris wiping their faces with filth as human ash floated by like pulverized flowers.

I'm not convinced that it makes more sense to be buried back East among rain-soaked earthworms in the cemetery across from the elementary school I graduated from, my flat chest pinned with a war-stamp corsage. My mother was always asking where I'd "end up," implying that I should finish a step higher, with reconciliation achieved. Yet here I am yearning for the Vedas of New—or Old—Age.

Where Do I Go?

Do I go into partnership with a friend who, between dowsing for water and then oil, wants me to replenish her cash flow by investing in her breeding attempts to bring back the unicorn? Her face darkens below a sequined baseball cap. Patiently, she explains that she has half a dozen

Arabian horses ready to be bred "into higher consciousness" through a combination of earth and water signs.

I think of the PBS show on the vanishing rhino, hunted by some as the lone-horned unicorn. I think of the *New Yorker* cover that followed up a sheep cloning by showing multiple sheep with the head of Einstein. I think of the lucky dogs getting an energy high from magnets, or bristling with quivering needles. They're soaring while I'm ever earth's Taurean, butting into walls.

I've also turned down a friend who wants me to invest in windmills. I'm a Quixote posing as a Santa Fe native who, while adopting the sombrero, pleated broomstick skirt, and cowboy boots, thinks she's kept her integrity by resisting a conch belt.

There's always levitation. But frankly, I can't afford a face or tummy lift.

So how does an agnostic—which is to an atheist as Unitarian is to Jewish—get God's attention? By fasting (with an ulcer), or staging a strike, or regressing to a past life of floating in brine? For anyone feeling flat as a pancake, it's not easy to deal with a Southwest that produces skyscraper-defying Navajos and peyote-chewing Cheyennes who don't choke on the smoke from a peace pipe.

If My Face Shows Some Mileage, I Must Have Learned a Thing or Two along the Road

Like any improper Bostonian, I started out between a rock and a hard place. At thirty, I took Valium. At forty, I took off my bra in the cause of sexual liberation. At fifty, I took a younger lover whose judgment was warped by marijuana. At sixty, I took a rest. What will I take at seventy—more blood-pressure tests?

Believe me, I've tried to break from the chain gang of Old Age. Had I not, you'd call me a complainer. A malcontent. One more voice in the *Oy Yoy* chorus. Another so-what who-cares?

I know you'll groan if I say that I've only questions, not answers. I punish myself with mental acupuncture. I pick holes in my brain. Is the pain real or virtual?

Next Stop, Millennium

I should be motivated, along with New Agers, by the mere mention of the year 2000. While I can't pass a religious litmus test and fear that I'm not truly spiritual, my prospects are actually thrilling. It will take a while to write the correct date on my checks. On bad days I tell Fate it's hard enough to deal with one new year, let alone 1,000 of them. And yet . . . a new millennium! This will never again happen to me, or to you.

Frankly, I don't see the world ending in 2000 C.E., or even in 2060, when some folks expect a mass migration to the twelfth planet. I believe that confused computers—with help from the federal bureaucracy—will solve their number bind. Earth will still be around, creaking in its orbit, neither more noticeably rusty nor more depraved. It may be a shade more polluted, like the Ganges. As long as I'm around, I'll be tormented by guilt that I hadn't evolved faster and further.

The New Millennium Must Bring a New Age

The new millennium is sure to usher in a flood of transformed consciousness in which Lucifer is drowned rather than the familiar trickle oozing from a cracked pipe. Palestinian and Israeli, Serb and Croat, Tutsi and Hutu will embrace without pulling a knife. Hunger will be erased if it is not co-opted by administrative costs. Immortality will abound. The year 2000 is a spaceship requiring New Age qualifications. Will I be left behind on the docking platform, Mother's voice in my ear chortling, *I told you so?*

The UFOs will have computers with strap-on face masks, joysticks, or floating gloves; massage tables; keyboard violins that play light-composed rap music or serve astronaut appetizers. I suspect that these ships will be virtual.

My quest rockets out into the unknown, its vessel shaped like a question mark. If there is a message here, it is simply this: *resist the tendency to be swept away.* Make up your own mind. Take control of your life.

Bruised by rolfing, you might be blessed with visions or left moaning for an ice pack. Away with mindless obedience to seductive fads.

Don't cease to question facile solutions. While examining turn-of-the-century panaceas, select what may be useful in your own life and appropriate to a global vision. Examine holistic products—including ideas—to see if they add to or subtract from the wholeness of an informed existence. Like the Mughal emperor Shah Jahan, let's weigh ourselves against our jewels, winnow out the genuine from the paste. In this way we can give to others and share in the bounty. The emperor regarded this spiritual fueling as charity; we call it networking to conserve our personal assets and to transform the earth's into lush, green valleys. Even to imagine spaceships transporting us into the immensity of the universe, we need to stretch to keep body and mind from stiffening into premature rigor mortis.

Approach judiciously all "new" ideas about nutrition. "Organic" is a dietary slogan plagiarizing the genes that glue us together; organic edibles may be corrupted by carelessness or market greed. Pollution of the earth by pesticides and nuclear fallout urges us to fight sanely against further inroads on its sanctity.

Insist on advertising that helps sort out what works for you from what does not. Take off the jazzy chakra clothing of holism, and thoughtfully examine the ancient carcass it conceals. Separate incense from common sense.

Last, but far from least, *refrain from the hysteria of millenarianism,* the tendency to stampede like buffalo over imaginary precipices. Skeptics of Colombus's mission visualized him going over the edge of a flat plane. What's the hurry? The clock should keep ticking without a pause into the millennia after Moses, Buddha, and Christ. If the battery fails, remind yourself that time, according to some ancients, is a myth, as are concepts of past, present, and future. Barring a nuclear accident or the onset of a new ice age, we should, undinosaurianly, continue apace.

May humor, wedded to critical thinking, prevail.

Glossary

Abs Colloquial for abdominal muscles—upper, lower, and outer.

Acupressure A set of body therapies similar to acupuncture, but relying on hand pressure rather than needles.

Acupuncture A method (originally Chinese) for treating various conditions by pricking the skin or tissue with gold or silver needles.

Age of Aquarius From astrology; in the Age of Aquarius the sun will be in the sign of Aquarius on the day of the spring equinox.

Alexander Technique Developed by Frederic Matthias Alexander; a form of reeducating an unbalanced body by concentrating on the head and neck, based on the theory that imbalance produces faulty breathing, spine distortion, and physical tensions.

Allopathic medicine The practice of treating disease by producing effects different from those produced by the disease.

Applied kinesiology A form of bodywork employing the use of muscle testing and acupressure to diagnose and treat physiological problems.

Aromatherapy The art of using aromatic oils extracted from plants to enhance physical and mental health.

Autism A mental condition, usually present from childhood, characterized by complete self-absorption and a reduced ability to respond to or communicate with the outside world.

Auto-da-fé A sentence of punishment enacted during the Spanish Inquisition; especially the burning of a heretic.

Avatar From Hindu mythology; a deity or soul that has descended to earth in bodily form.

Ayurvedic A Hindu system of medicine based largely on principles Westerners associate with homeopathy and naturopathy.

Bach Flower Remedies Originated by Edward Bach; extracts of plants originally found to produce cures corresponding to basic personality types.

Beta-carotene A vitamin A supplement alleged to have immune-enhancing action.

Biofeedback A technique for monitoring an automatic bodily response to a stimulus in order to acquire voluntary control of that response.

Biorhythms Biological cycles usually existing since birth and found to follow a sine curve. Positive cycles cause enhancement of talents; negative cycles have the opposite effect. Accidents are thought to occur on "critical" days when cycles cross the zero line or intersect one another.

Black Tara   One of twenty-one Buddhist expressions of Tara, daughter of the usually male Avalokitesvara (Guanyin), Bodhisattva of Infinite Compassion. These goddesses have different colors, postures, and attributes, and are either peaceful or warlike. The most popular ones are White Tara and Green Tara.

Bodhisattva   From Mahayana Buddhism; a savior who delays passage to Nirvana out of compassion for human suffering.

Cayce, Edgar   An early-twentieth-century clairvoyant who gave psychic readings on health and reincarnation.

Chakras   Seven bodily centers of spiritual energy perceptible to clairvoyants.

Channeling   A process used to access and express information from a nonordinary consciousness source via verbal presentation or automatic writing.

Ch'i   A Chinese word meaning vital energy, or breath.

Chinese Medicine   A traditional therapeutic approach based on acu-puncture, acupressure, and herbs.

Chiropractic   An alternative medical treatment developed in 1913 by Daniel David Palmer, based on the belief that the body can maintain well-being through manipulation of the spinal column.

Chopra, Deepak   A popular New Age author and TV personality; physician-director of San Diego's Sharp Institute for Human Potential and Mind-Body Medicine.

Chutzpa   A Yiddish word meaning brazenness, shamelessness, gall.

Clairvoyance The faculty of perceiving things or events in the future, or free of normal sensory contact.

A Course in Miracles A nearly 1,200-page channeled document recorded by Helen Schucman in 1965 and first published in 1975. See Williamson, Marianne.

Crystals Stones believed to be invested with magical or occult properties, or with healing powers.

Cveching Yiddish word that means complaining.

Dharma Buddhist truth; also Hindu social or moral law.

DNA (Dioxyribonucleic acid) A self-replicating constituent of chromosomes; the carrier of genetic information present in living organisms.

Doppelganger An apparition, or double, of a living person.

Dowsing Probing for a source of water or minerals with a divining rod.

Dybbuk A malevolent spirit in Jewish folklore.

Empirical Based on observation or experiment, as opposed to theory.

Esalen Institute An educational establishment founded by Michael Murphy and Richard Price at Big Sur, California, in 1962. Courses and seminars have included Comparative Religion, Group Awareness, Emotional Re-Education, Expansion of Consciousness, and innovative approaches to health care and treatment of the mentally ill.

Feng shui The Chinese geomantic art of designing healthful living and working environments. See Geomancy.

Freemason Member of an international society for mutual help and fellowship, long believed to be in possession of ancient knowledge used in the construction of sacred buildings and monuments.

Geomancy Divination derived from the earth's configurations.

Gnostic Occult; mystic.

Goyisch Yiddish for Gentile, a person of non-Jewish descent.

Hallucinogens Drugs causing hallucinations.

Harmonic Convergence The prediction that a strong cosmic force will peak through the collective energy projected by human thought.

Hippocratic Related to a system of medicine founded by Hippocrates in fifth-century B.C.E. Greece.

Holistic health A system of beliefs based on the premise that wellness proceeds from a harmonic balance of physical, mental, and emotional processes.

Hologram From physics; a three-dimensional image formed by the interference of light beams from a coherent light source.

Homeopathy A therapeutic approach founded in the early nineteenth century by Samuel Hahnemann in which minute doses of substances producing symptoms in a healthy person will cure those symptoms in one who is ill.

Humours The four chief fluids of the body: blood, phlegm, choler, and melancholy.

Hydrotherapy A healing approach based on the theory that harmony with nature is effected through water or dry cures.

Hypnosis A process that leads to altered states of consciousness ranging from a light trance to catalepsy, and characterized by varying degrees of suggestibility, dissociation, amnesia, or anesthesia.

Incubi Evil spirits that descend on sleeping people.

Integral Yoga A form of yoga introduced by Sri Aurobindo in the early twentieth century.

Jin Shin Do The art of universal energy developed in recent decades by Ron and Iona Teegarten from an ancient healing method known as Jin Shin Jyutsu, which calls for the use of hands instead of needles on acupuncture points. Jin Shin Do follows the same basic tenets, with the addition of yogic breathing techniques, exercise, and meditation.

Kabbala The Jewish mystical tradition; also, the compilation of such teachings.

Karma A Buddhist and Hindu term indicating the sum of a person's actions in previous states of existence that influence the individual's fate in future lives.

Ketones Any of a class of organic compounds formed when the body has been burning proteins and fats; found in the blood and urine of diabetics with impaired metabolism.

Kundalini yoga A form of yogic practice aimed at moving "serpent energy" from the base of the spine to the crown of the head to awaken a state of bliss.

Lao-tzu The sixth-century B.C.E. founder of Taoism, a Chinese philosophy espousing the Natural Way, nature transforming itself, and the concept of nonbeing, or nothingness.

Laser A device that generates an intense beam of coherent mono-chromatic radiation in the infrared, visible, or ultraviolet region of the electromagnetic spectrum through the stimulated emission of photons from an excited source.

Levitation Rising, or causing to float in the air.

Living Will A signed, dated, and witnessed document authorizing in advance the withholding or withdrawal of artificial life-support (in some states, "death-defying") measures in the event of a terminal illness or injury.

Macrobiotics A diet devised by George Ohsawa in the mid-1960s to prolong life and consisting of regimens of pure vegetable foods and unpolished brown rice, along with spiritual precepts based on ancient Japanese beliefs and practices.

Mantra A word or sound repeated to aid concentration in meditation.

Massage The art of treating ailments through the manipulation of muscles and joints; an aspect of bodywork.

Materia medica The remedial substances used in the practice of medicine.

Meditation Spiritual exercises to steer normal waking consciousness in a more positive direction.

Medium A person claiming to be in contact with spirits of the dead and to communicate between the dead and the living.

Neoplatonism A philosophical and religious system combining Platonic thought with Eastern mysticism.

Network A loose structure of people or groups with shared interests.

Nirvana The Buddhist place or state of perfect bliss and release from Karma, attained by the extinction of individuality.

Orgone A form of cosmic energy discovered by Wilhelm Reich in the late 1930s and used to treat diseases, especially cancer, by way of an orgone accumulator box.

Palmistry Divination derived through lines and other features on the palm of the hand.

Paradigm An example or pattern.

Paranormal Beyond the scope of normal objective investigation or explanation.

Parrish-Hanna, Carol Founder of Sparrow Hawk Spiritual Community—a New Age model commune—and pastor of the Light of Christ Community Church in Tahlequah, Oklahoma; known as a walk-in, a soul that takes over an unwanted body.

Past-life therapy The use of bodywork and hypnosis to uncover previous existences.

Phrenology Divination derived through the study of skull conformation.

Poltergeist A noisy, mischievous ghost.

Pranayama Yogic breath control.

Precognition Foreknowledge of a supernatural kind.

Psychometry The divination of facts about events and people from inanimate objects associated with them.

Pythagorean   Related to Pythagoras, sixth-century B.C.E. Greek philosopher who instructed students in the transmigration of souls.

Ram Dass, Baba (Richard Alpert)   New Age teacher, author, founder of The Hanuman Foundation; spiritual leader at the end of the 1960s.

Rebirthing   A transformational process used to identify and isolate areas in consciousness that trigger present-day problems.

Reflexology (also Zone therapy or Foot therapy)   A form of bodywork based on stroking or applying pressure to body zones, especially in the foot.

Reiki   An art of promoting universal life energy to foster healing through hand placement.

Reincarnation   The belief that the soul passes from one body to another in a series of earth-plane existences.

Der Ring des Nibelungen   *The Ring of the Nibelungen,* a stage-festival play with words and music by Richard Wagner, and consisting of four operas: "Das Rheingold," "Die Walküre," "Siegfried," and "Götterdämmerung."

Rolfing   A bodywork technique devised by Ida R. Rolf in the mid-twentieth century and based on heavy manipulation of deep connective body tissue between bone joints.

Rosicrucian   Member of a society devoted to the study of metaphysical and mystical lore, most prevalent in the seventeenth and eighteenth centuries.

Shamanism   An age-old healing discipline that involves journeying to other realms to bring back lost portions of the soul and guiding souls of the dead to their home in the afterlife.

Shiatsu A form of acupressure rooted in Japanese *amma* massage.

Shtick A Yiddish word meaning gimmick.

Succubi Female demons that have intercourse with sleeping men.

Swedenborgian Related to Emmanuel Swedenborg, eighteenth-century philosopher, biblical scholar, and mystic who synthesized religion and mystical thought.

Synergic The efforts of agents such as drugs that, when combined, produce a total effect greater than the sum of the individual elements.

Tarot A pack of cards used in fortune-telling.

Tautology The repetition of something in different words, usually reflecting a fault in style.

Telepathy Communication of thoughts or ideas other than through the known senses.

Thanatological Pertaining to the scientific study of death, including its causes and phenomena, the effects of approaching death, and the words of the terminally ill and their families.

Theosophical Society An organization founded in 1875 by Helena Petrovna Blavatsky to pass on occult traditions related to universal brotherhood in North America and Europe.

Theurgy Supernatural or divine agency in human affairs.

UFO (Unidentified flying object) One of numerous space-ships first reported in the United States after an alleged sighting in 1947; believed by some to be inhabited by extraterrestrial humanoids.

Williamson, Marianne A contemporary author and well-known disseminator of ideas promoted in *A Course in Miracles*.

Wraith A ghost or apparition.

Zoroastrian A follower of Zoroaster's dualistic religious system based on conflict between spirits of light (good) and spirits of darkness (evil). Founded in the fifth century B.C.E. on the teachings of the prophet Zarathustra, Zoroastrianism was the dominant religion of Persia for more than 1,000 years.

Notes

Chapter One

1. Marilyn Ferguson, *The Aquarian Conspiracy: Personal and Social Transformation in the 1980s* (Los Angeles: J. P. Tarcher, 1980), p. 27.
2. René Daumal, *Mount Analogue* (Baltimore, MD: Penguin Books, 1974), p. 185.
3. *Santa Fe Sun* (December 1997).
4. Ram Dass, "Immortality of the Soul," *The Holistic Health Lifebook: A Guide to Personal and Planetary Well-Being,* by Berkeley Holistic Health Center (Berkeley, CA: And/Or Press, 1981), pp. 202–203.
5. Levi, *The Aquarian Gospel of Jesus the Christ: The Philosophic and Practical Basis of the Religion of the Aquarian Age of the World* (Los Angeles: Leo W. Dowling, 1930), p. 7.

Chapter Two

1. Genesis 17:17.
2. Luke 1:36.

3. Barbara G. Walker, *The Crone: Woman of Age, Wisdom, and Power* (New York: Harper Collins, 1985), p. 119.

Chapter Three

1. Herbert D. Puryear, *The Edgar Cayce Primer: Discovering the Path to Self-Transformation* (New York: Bantam Books, 1986), p. 87.
2. Ibid., p. 66.
3. Deepak Chopra, *Journey into Healing: Awakening the Wisdom within You* (New York: Crown, 1994), p. 7.
4. Ibid., p. 144.
5. Ibid., p. 145.
6. Marianne Williamson, *A Return to Love: Reflections on the Principles of A Course in Miracles* (New York: Harper Collins, 1992), p. 110.
7. Ibid., p. 150.
8. Ibid., p. 227.
9. See Note 3, p. 40.

Chapter Four

1. Gillian Bennett, *Traditions of Belief* (London, England: Penguin Books, 1987), p. 167.
2. Ibid., p. 37.
3. Aldous Huxley, *The Devils of Loudon* (New York: Harper & Row, 1971), p. 173.
4. Barbara G. Walker, *The Crone: Woman of Age, Wisdom, and Power* (New York: Harper Collins, 1985), p. 132.
5. Ibid., p. 129.
6. Author undocumented, *Demoniolatry* (Paris, France: L. Sinistrari, 1879).
7. See Note 3, p. 175.

Chapter Five

1. Arthur C. Hastings, PhD, James Fadiman, PhD, and James S. Gordon, MD, *Health for the Whole Person: The Complete Guide to Holistic Medicine* (Boulder, CO: Westview Press, 1980), p. 23.
2. Marilyn Ferguson, "A New Perspective on Reality," *The Holistic Health Lifebook: A Guide to Personal and Planetary Well-Being,* by Berkeley Holistic Health Center (Berkeley, CA: And/Or Press, 1981), p. 185.
3. Ibid., p. 102.
4. Deepak Chopra, *Journey into Healing: Awakening the Wisdom within You* (New York: Crown, 1994), p. 142.

Chapter Seven

1. Aldous Huxley, *The Devils of Loudon* (New York: Harper & Row, 1971), p. 170.

Chapter Twelve

1. David van Bhema, "Does Heaven Exist?" *Time* (24 March 1997): 75.
2. Jeffrey Burton Russell, *A History of Heaven: The Singing Silence* (Princeton, NJ: Princeton University Press, 1997).

Chapter Fourteen

1. Howard Rheingold, *Virtual Reality* (New York: Summit Books, 1991), pp. 15–16.
2. Ibid., p. 256.
3. Ibid., p. 262.
4. Susumu Tachi, quoted in Howard Rheingold, *Virtual Reality* (New York: Summit Books, 1991), p. 264.
5. See Note 1, p. 271.
6. See Note 1, p. 272.

Chapter Fifteen

1. English-Lueck, J. A. (June Ann), *Health in the New Age: A Study in California Holistic Practices* (Albuquerque, NM: University of New Mexico Press, 1990), pp. 109–110.
2. Aldous Huxley, *The Devils of Loudon* (New York: Harper & Row, 1971), pp. 356–357.
3. Ibid., p. 157.
4. Robin Wright, Ronald R. Ostrow, and Marlene Cimons, "America Is Increasingly Vulnerable to Terrorism," *Urban Terrorism* (San Diego, CA: Greenhaven Press, 1996), pp. 18–21; Adam Goprick, "America's Violent Culture Leads to Terrorism," *Urban Terrorism* (San Diego, CA: Greenhaven Press, 1996), pp. 22–26; and Thomas Powers, "American Violence Does Not Lead to Terrorism," *Urban Terrorism* (San Diego, CA: Greenhaven Press, 1996), pp. 30–31.

Chapter Sixteen

1. *The New York Times* (21 September 1988): A-11.
2. Jerry Mander, *In the Absence of the Sacred: The Failure of Technology and the Survival of the Indian Nations* (San Francisco: Sierra Club Books, 1991), p. 223.
3. Ibid.
4. Barbara G. Walker, *The Crone: Woman of Age, Wisdom, and Power* (New York: Harper Collins, 1985), p. 51.
5. See Note 2, p. 245.
6. See Note 4, p. 64.
7. Paolo Soleri, *Arcology: The City in the Image of Man* (Cambridge, MA: MIT Press, 1969), preface to the paperback edition.
8. Paolo Soleri, *The Bridge between Matter & Spirit Is Matter Becoming Spirit: The Arcology of Paolo Soleri* (Garden City, NY: Anchor Books, 1973), p. 43.
9. See Note 7.
10. Alfred Bernhart, quoted in *Sacred Space: Meaning and Form,* ed. by

David James Randolph (New York: United Chirch Board for Homeland Ministries, 1976), p. 87.

11. Dan Fagin, Marianne Lavelle, and the Center for Public Integrity, *Toxic Deception: How the Chemical Industry Manipulates Science, Bends the Law, and Endangers Your Health* (Secaucus, NJ: Birch Lane Press, 1996).

12. Parvati Markus, in *Santa Fe Sun* (August 1997): 13.

13. Barbara G. Walker, *The Crone: Woman of Age, Wisdom, and Power* (New York: Harper Collins, 1985), p. 63.

14. Antonio Lopez, in *Santa Fe Sun* (August 1997): 10.

Chapter Seventeen

1. Marilyn Ferguson, *The Aquarian Conspiracy: Personal and Social Transformation in the 1980s* (Los Angeles: J. P. Tarcher, 1980), p. 218.

2. Eva Wong, *Feng-shui: The Ancient Wisdom of Harmonious Living for Modern Times* (New York: Shambhala, 1966), p. 10.

3. George Trevelyan, *A Vision of the Aquarian Age: The Emerging Spiritual World View* (London, England: Coventure, Ltd., 1984), p. 168.

Recommended Reading

Books

Airola, Paavo O. *How to Keep Slim, Healthy and Young with Juice Fasting*. Phoenix, AZ: Health Plus, 1971.

Bauman, Edward, Armand Bint, Loren Piper, Amelia Wright, and the Berkeley Holistic Health Center. *The Holistic Health Lifebook: A Guide to Personal and Planetary Well-Being*. Berkeley, CA: And/Or Press, 1981.

Bennett, Gillian. *Traditions of Belief: Women, Folklore and the Supernatural Today*. London, England: Penguin Books, 1987.

Chopra, Deepak, MD. *Journey into Healing: Awakening the Wisdom within You*. New York: Harmony Books, 1994.

Corcoran, Bobbi. *The New Age Community Guidebook: Alternative Choices in Lifestyles*. Middletown, CA: Harbin Springs Publishing, 1989.

A Course in Miracles, vol. 2. Tiburon, CA: Foundation for Inner Peace, 1975.

Diamond, Harvey and Marilyn. *Fit for Life*. New York: Warner Books, 1985.

English-Lueck, J. A. (June Ann). *Health in the New Age: A Study in California Holistic Practices.* Albuquerque, NM: University of New Mexico Press, 1990.

Fagin, Dan, Marianne Lavelle, and the Center for Public Integrity. *Toxic Deception: How the Chemical Industry Manipulates Science, Bends the Law, and Endangers Your Health.* Secaucus, NJ: Birch Lane Press, 1996.

Ferguson, Marilyn. *The Aquarian Conspiracy: Personal and Social Transformation in the 1980s.* Los Angeles: J. P. Tarcher, 1980.

Graedon, Joe and Teresa. *50+: The Graedons' People's Pharmacy for Older Adults.* New York: Bantam Books, 1988.

Gray, William D. *Thinking Critically about New Age Ideas.* Belmont, CA: Wadsworth Publishing, 1991.

Hastings, Arthur C., PhD, James C. Fadiman, PhD, James S. Gordon, MD. *Health for the Whole Person: The Complete Guide to Holistic Medicine.* Boulder, CO: Westview Press, 1980.

Huxley, Aldous. *The Devils of Loudon.* New York: Harper & Row, 1971.

Levi. *The Aquarian Gospel of Jesus the Christ: The Philosophic and Practical Basis of the Religion of the Aquarian Age of the World.* Los Angeles: Leo W. Dowling, 1930.

Lifespan-plus: 900 Natural Techniques to Live Longer. Ed. by the editors of *Prevention Magazine.* Emmaus, PA: Rodale Press, 1990.

MacLaine, Shirley. *Dancing in the Light.* New York: Bantam Books, 1985.

Mander, Jerry. *In the Absence of the Sacred: The Failure of Technology and the Survival of the Indian Nations.* San Francisco: Sierra Club Books, 1991.

Melton, James Gordon. *New Age Encyclopedia.* Detroit, MI: Gale Research, 1990.

The New Consciousness Sourcebook. Berkeley, CA: Arcline Publications, 1984.

Parrish-Harra, Carol W. *A New Age Handbook for Death and Dying.* Marina del Rey, CA: DeVorss & Company, 1982.

Puryear, Herbert D. *The Edgar Cayce Primer: Discovering the Path to Self-Transformation.* New York: Bantam Books,. 1986.

Rheingold, Howard. *Virtual Reality*. New York: Summit Books, 1991.

Ross, Shirley. *Fasting: The Super Diet*. New York: Ballantine Books, 1976.

Rosten, Leo Calvin. *Hooray for Yiddish: A Book about English*. New York: Simon & Schuster, 1982.

Sacred Space: Meaning and Form. Ed. by David James Randolph. The International Congress on Religion, Architecture and the Arts. New York: United Church Board for Homeland Ministries, 1976.

Trevelyan, George. *A Vision of the Aquarian Age: The Emerging Spiritual World View*. London, England: Coventure, Ltd., 1984.

Urban Terrorism. San Diego, CA: Greenhaven Press, 1996.

Walker, Barbara G. *The Crone: Woman of Age, Wisdom, and Power*. New York: Harper Collins, 1985.

Williamson, Marianne. *A Return to Love: Reflections on the Principles of A Course in Miracles*. New York: Harper Collins, 1992.

Wong, Eva. *Feng-shui: The Ancient Wisdom of Harmonious Living for Modern Times*. New York: Shambhala, 1966.

Periodicals and Catalogs

Elderhostel: United States and Canada Catalog (Winter 1997).

Life Magazine (July 1997): 39–52.

Santa Fe Sun (August 1997 and December 1997).

About the Author

Arlene Stone is a feminist antiwar activist who has swum her way around the globe from Boston to Beijing and from St. Peter's to St. Petersburg, trying to make sense of a world that veers between insanity and inanity. Mother of two grown children, her hobbies are travel, reading, and nagging others to act on behalf of peace.

Newly rooted in Santa Fe, New Mexico, Ms. Stone is à zeppelin craving to be refitted for planetary travel, a crystal that while capable of critical thinking, is just as likely to be bewitched by the smoky mirrors of poetry. At sixty-plus, she flaunts crazy hats and won't slow down until all weapons of war have been recycled into habitations for the homeless.

Order Form

Quantity		Amount
_____	*Old Age in the New Age: Irreverent Reflections on Millennial Madness* ($14.95)	_____
	Sales tax of 6.25% for New Mexico residents	_____
	Shipping & handling ($2.70; plus $1.00 per book on orders of two or more)	_____
	Total amount enclosed	_____

Quantity discounts available

Please photocopy this order form, fill it out, and mail it, together with your personal check or money order (US currency only) to:

Optimist Press
PO Box 2880
Santa Fe, NM 87504-2880
505-820-6511